VIKING FUND PUBLICATIONS IN ANTHROPOLOGY

Number Fifty-two   Colin M. Turnbull, *Editor*

Anthropology, History, and Cultural Change

Margaret T. Hodgen

Published for the Wenner-Gren Foundation for Anthropological Research Inc.

The University of Arizona Press   Tucson, Arizona

About the Author . . .

MARGARET T. HODGEN, once Fellow of the Henry E. Huntington Library and of the John Simon Guggenheim Memorial Foundation, for many years was a member of the teaching staff of the Department of Social Institutions at the University of California in Berkeley, holding the chairmanship of the department for eight of those years. A frequent contributor to scholarly journals in anthropology and related fields, she also is the author of *The Doctrine of Survivals: A History of Scientific Method in the Study of Man* (1933); *Change and History: A Study of the Dated Distributions of Technological Innovations in England* (1952); and *Early Anthropology in the Sixteenth and Seventeenth Centuries* (1964).

THE UNIVERSITY OF ARIZONA PRESS

Copyright © 1974
Wenner-Gren Foundation for Anthropological Research, Inc.
All Rights Reserved
Manufactured in the U.S.A.

I.S.B.N.-0-8165-0451-2
L.C. No. 74-77208

Contents

List of Tables

Chart

List of Maps

Preface

Although it has been said that the mere mention of a theory of social change "will make most social scientists appear defensive, furtive, guilt-ridden, or frightened," this social process—its place, rate, and description—is nevertheless one of the most frequently avowed interests of both historians and anthropologists. On the paramount importance of this problem, the two disciplines are united. It is only on the means by which a solution is to be reached that divisiveness appears. By tradition each goes its own way, uninformed and incurious concerning the similarities of some of their methodological ideas as well as their differences. Historians, for the most part, deny the likenesses observable in many categories of dated cultural changes. Advised by philosophers, they regard dated events as unique and resistant to classification. On the other hand, anthropology so far has tended to confine its inquiries to the nonliterate and nonhistorical peoples. Anthropological treatment of the temporal aspect of cultural changes is seldom guided by the study of dated changes. It relies upon various theories of diffusion, the paradigms of development or evolution, or the imposition on the unstudied past of conclusions reached concerning cultural changes in the present ceaselessly replicated.

The following pages are an expansion of these and other observations. They contain a suggested alternative approach involving the acceptance of the likeness of at least some dated changes, their classification and comparison, accompanied by a few obvious inferences.

CHAPTER 1

Anthropologists and Historians: Their Attitudes Toward the Use of Scientific Method

Several tasks of singular importance confront inquirers in the social studies in this latter third of the twentieth century. One, perhaps the most important, is to find a means of dissolving the interdisciplinary conflicts and overlappings which confuse investigators and burden the budget. Since, in many instances, these barriers between fields of study are the result of the acceptance of traditional and unexamined methodological assumptions, or paradigms, inherited from the eighteenth and earlier centuries, it would seem that the centrifugal effects of specialization could best be diminished by a search for a newly evaluated, clearly apprehended, and common body of organizing principles. This re-evaluation should take into account that mankind, the common object of study in all the social sciences is uniquely a member of two worlds: the undated natural world (restricted by its undatedness to the study of the present in field or laboratory) and the dated world with its access to dated records of the human past as well as the human present.

Mankind, as a member of the natural world, the world of laboratory experimentation, mathematics, computers, and the statement of natural laws, has received the unremitting attention of social scientists for many years. He has supposedly been exhaustively subjected to scientific method. Many social disciplines, as a result, are well on the way to sophisticated conclusions concerning man as he exists today, or existed in his past, by the extrapolation of results arrived at in the laboratory. To the historically, or even scientifically, minded, however, the recovery of the human past by extrapolation seems unnecessarily conjectural. One wonders why, in the study of man, as in the study of geology,[1] vast stores of chronological or dated material cannot also be subjected to scientific method. It is suggested here that scientific method *can* be applied to chronological or dated material if only inherited and traditional organizing ideas be re-examined, and when necessary or possible, replaced with others more appropriate to this newer undertaking.

The relevance of these remarks may be judged by considering some of the procedures commonly employed in anthropology and history; for these two social disciplines together claim sovereignty over the study of human activity, both temporal and spatial. They include, as subjects of study, man primitive and preliterate, man literate and civilized, man historyless and man historical. By what traditional barriers then are they now separated? By what modifications of organizing principles could they be brought together for the advancement of knowledge? Obviously before each can cooperate with the other, or even wisely use the findings of the other, it is necessary for each to understand what the other considers to be its problem, and how it approaches a solution. Unless the social anthropologist informs himself realistically concerning the historian's view of dated events and the narrative, serial structure into which these events are thrown, unless the historian knows how the anthropologist reaches his conclusions, there can be no reconciliation between the descriptive interests of the one and the temporal interests of the other.

It will clarify discussion if it be said at once that anthropology is not primarily a form of historical inquiry. It is usually considered a natural science,[2] descriptive, morphological, and classificatory— similar in everything except its primary subject matter (the preliterate cultures of mankind) to the procedures of botanists and zoologists. This was made clear, a century and a half ago, in 1839 at the Birmingham meeting of the British Association for the Advancement of Science

1. See, for example, the works of George Gaylord Simpson for expositions of the techniques and methods adopted by a geologist in applying the method of science to dated or temporally arrangeable materials.

2. Anthropology "has been rather freely admitted by scientists to fall within the domain of natural science" (Alfred Louis Kroeber, *Configurations of culture growth*, 3). "It is plain that such a large part of the area of knowledge as the humanities control cannot be permanently reserved as outside natural science. Man *is* in nature even if he does also have a history" (Alfred Louis Kroeber, "Integration of the knowledge of man," 127). The view of the social anthropologist, Evans-Pritchard is different: "It is easy to define the aim of the social anthropologist to be the establishment of sociological laws, but nothing remotely resembling a law of the natural sciences has yet been adduced . . . social anthropology is a kind of historiography . . . it studies societies as moral systems not as natural systems" (E. E. Evans-Pritchard, "Social anthropology: past and present," 20, 26).

where a social science, "ethnography," first came under discussion before the Natural Historical Section. There, Dr. James C. Prichard (1786-1848) stressed the immediate need for obtaining descriptions of the physical characters of the "threatened," or fast disappearing, races and proposed that a questionnaire be carried by travellers instructing them to make inquiries among such people concerning their languages, family life, sports and amusements, ceremonies, foods, dress, treatment of the sick, funerals, works of art, government, laws, and religion. This plan, it was said, "need not equal in expense what is often done for other objects of zoology and botany."[3]

A similar concept of the aims of ethnology was expressed a generation later by Sir Edward Burnett Tylor (1832-1917) in his *Primitive Culture,* published in 1871.[4] "Just as the catalogue of all the species of plants and animals of a district represents its Flora and Fauna, so the list of all the items of the general life of the people represents that whole which we call its culture." These items, Tylor said further, were to be dissected into details and classified in their proper groups. This done, however, the work of the anthropologist, as a naturalist, was not complete. It had yet to be decided whether that perennial historical problem of botany and zoology, the problem of change in past time, could be solved in the study of culture. In Tylor's words, inquiry had to find out "how the facts in these groups are produced by evolution from one another," acknowledging meanwhile that it was "an open question whether the theory of development[5] from species to species is a record of transition which actually took place, or a mere ideal scheme. . . ."

A second tie with natural science was woven into the structure of anthropological thought through what had become known over the years as the problem of civilization. So stated, and whatever its earlier solutions,[6] it was solved satisfactorily for Tylor and genera-tions of successors by recourse to the eighteenth-century theory of social progress (by him also called development or evolution) and by the hierarchical arrangement of existing primitive systems of behavior and those "higher" cultures known to history in the order

3. Report of the 11th Meeting of the British Association for the Advancement of Science held at Plymouth in July 1841, 52-55, 332-39.
4. Sir Edward Burnett Tylor, *Primitive culture,* I: 8, 7, 4.
5. Or what, in more modern terminology, might be called "the paradigm" of development.
6. For the Renaissance problem of civilization, see Margaret T. Hodgen, *Early anthropology in the sixteenth and seventeenth centuries,* 256, 288, 462-63. For recent treatments of the problem of civilization, see, for example, Toynbee and Kroeber.

of their temporal appearance.[7] As a result, everyone is familiar with the countless efforts made by enthusiasts to recover cultural origins with what was then called the Comparative[8] or Historical Method, and with the construction of innumerable stage series purporting to exhibit in macrocosmic dimensions the natural course of cultural change in past time.

Following Dr. James C. Prichard, Tylor and others, anthropology has become more and more narrowly concerned with the study of preliterate peoples. This steadfastness may be regarded as both a necessity and an instance of academic habit. The destructive impact of western culture upon the primitive way of life has compelled haste in the collection of descriptions of existing primitive cultures. On the other hand, the amassment of such materials,[9] together with pressure for their classification, has discouraged radical departures from earlier interests and basic procedures. Although a few anthropologists have ventured to address themselves to the description of some advanced, historical cultures,[10] the *pasts* of these peoples have not been subjected to anthropological investigation; nor has inquiry into the processes of cultural change been carried into a literature where dated changes and dated evidence are available.[11] Debate among anthropologists on their relationship to historians has seldom emerged, nor, with certain exceptions, have anthropologists been concerned with the use of scientific method on dated historical and cultural material. Although diffusionists have experimented with the determination of the chronology of *undated* traits (usually on the basis of

7. "It is desirable to work out as systematically as possible a scheme of evolution" or "to sketch a theoretical course of civilization . . . by comparing the various stages of civilization among races known to history" (Tylor, *Primitive culture*, I: 21). For this type of comparison, known in anthropology as the Comparative Method, see Frederick John Teggart, *Theory and processes of history*, 93-98, 102-109, 172, 282; Kenneth E. Bock, *The acceptance of histories*, 1-132.

8. Not to be confused with the use of comparison as an element in scientific method. See Kenneth E. Bock, "The comparative method of anthropology," 269-280.

9. "In sheer bulk the mass of descriptive material of interest to the anthropologist probably exceeds by several times that of all the rest of the social sciences put together" (George P. Murdock, "The processing of anthropological materials," 265).

10. David G. Mandelbaum, "The study of complex civilizations," 203-225. This discussion concentrates on the work of Kroeber, Benedict, and Mead, but mentions others. See also Clyde Kay Maben Kluckhohn, "Developments in the field of anthropology in the 20th century," 764-65; Robert T. Anderson, "Anthropology and history," 1-8; and Walter Goldschmidt, "The anthropological study of modern society," I, 330-39.

11. "In recent decades there has been an inclination to shift ethnographic studies from . . . nonliterates and primitives to . . . communities within literate civilizations. But . . . it is evident that this is a transfer of method; the inquiry remains face-to-face, not historical" (Kroeber, "What ethnography is," 136).

the age-and-area theory borrowed from botany and zoology)[12] anthropology has remained a descriptive inquiry concentrated upon a fraction of mankind—a fraction, preliterate, historyless, and dateless.[13]

But if, for these reasons, the anthropologist has appeared reluctant to form an interdisciplinary alliance with the historian, to deal with the historical cultures, or to take advantage, in the study of social change, of the historian's assets in the form of dated evidence, it must be acknowledged that the historians have not made cooperation easy. In the first place, "history" as a form of inquiry has been directed, not toward the past of man alone, but toward a confusing multiplicity of historical objects. Moreover, there is a singular lack of agreement among those who reconstruct the past of these various historical objects as to what they do when they write or compile histories. The historian, who takes mankind or some single human group, as an historical object, views it and the procedure required in one way.[14] The historical geologist views his objects of interest and methods in another. While the historian, as a naturalist or evolutionist, employs still other organizing principles.[15]

Nor is interdisciplinary exchange made any easier by the word "history" itself. In nearly all languages it is a double-barreled term, meaning both what has happened and the historian's statement of what has happened. In English, the situation is even more ambiguous. History is an overworked word, clouded with many meanings,[16] for

12. Some botanists and zoologists, when confronted with an area bearing different species may assume that, moving out from a center, the newest or most recent appears on the circumference, the oldest at the center, or vice versa. See Edward Sapir's masterful analysis of procedures designed to give temporal depth to undated distributions in *Time perspective in aboriginal American culture*.

13. To some anthropologists, "the growth of a general understanding of cultural change has seemed slow and unsatisfactory. There is widespread feeling that we have no really useful concepts, that there is no theory worthy of the name, for comparing and understanding the many instances of change with which we are acquainted" (*Perspectives in American Indian culture*, edited by Edward H. Spicer, 517).

14. For a short bibliography on history and ethnology, see Kluckhohn, "Anthropology in the 20th century," 768-72.

15. For a recent view of the relationship between "history" and the other studies of man, the social sciences, see Richard D. Challener and Maurice Lee, Jr., "History and the social sciences," 331-32.

16. The word *history* is used in at least five overlapping senses: (1) the systematic study of, or a treatise dealing with, natural phenomena—as in "natural history" or "life history"; (2) the past of mankind (or any part thereof); (3) the survivals and records of the past of mankind (or any part thereof)—as in "recorded history," "a history book," or "a case history"; (4) the study, representation, and explanation of the past of mankind (or any part thereof)—as in "written or spoken history"; and (5) the branch of knowledge that records, studies, represents, and explains the past of mankind (or any parts thereof)—as in "department of history," or "school of history" (*Theory and practice in historical study*, 133; see also pp. 127-128).

the performance of multiple divergent services. It may be used merely as a synonym for "the past," when it is said, for example, that "history" or "the past" has much to teach the present. It may refer to that vast, varied, and chaotic body of datable material, or, in the case of archaeology, to the temporally arrangeable artifacts and other documentation of the past available for "historical uses." It may call to mind the finished products of divergent kinds of historical inquiry: the dated historical narrative of a student of English history; the more limited temporal horizon of a writer of a monograph on the federal treatment of the Cherokee Indians; the ambitious compiler of a world history; the student of natural or evolutionary history in the fields of botany, zoology, and geology; or finally, all the books which line the shelves of the so-called historical subjects, or subjects "historically treated." These include, to name only a few, histories of law, land tenure, medicine, cosmetics, technology, commerce, ideas, language, the peasants, burgers, elite, the military, printing, the state, Christianity, the plow, the windmill, the history of science and the history of history itself. Obviously, everything in the world has a history in the sense of having a past; but the ways in which professional historians and others reconstruct these several pasts depend upon their objects of interest, and the mental habits or traditions of their academic predecessors or colleagues.

The reflective social anthropologist will know, as does also the historian, that what unifies all of these historical inquiries directed at so many different historical objects, and makes them "history," is the inquirer's conviction of the explanatory powers of the recovery of the past; the recovery of the past in serial form; and the conceptual endowment of such historical series with the ancient idea of genetic [17] or temporal connection among its dated members or events, which often, according to Marc Bloch, "confuse ancestry with explanation." [18]

17. "A genealogy has three elements: a person present or spoken of; a series of a series of ancestors; and a specific 'first' individual, source, or origin. . . . In the hands of the earlier Greeks . . . the genealogical method provided a form into which could be fitted an explanation either of a situation in the affairs of men or of a condition of things in the world of nature" (Teggart, *Theory and processes*, 82–84). For its use in nineteenth century biology, see Charles Darwin's remark in *The origin of species* that from the most remote period in the history of the world, "organized beings have been found to resemble each other in descending degrees, so that they can be classed in groups under groups. . . . I believe that the arrangement of the groups in each class . . . must be strictly genealogical to be natural. . . . Thus . . . the natural system (of classification) is genealogical in its arrangement, like a pedigree . . . . " (Charles Darwin, *The origin of species*, 411, 420, 422. See also Sidney Hook, "A pragmatic criticism of the historico-genetic method," and the discussion of Hook in John Herman Randall, Jr., *Nature and historical experience*, 65, 66.)

18. Marc Bloch, *The historian's craft*, 32.

These temporal series are arrived at in several ways depending upon whether the student is a conventional narrative historian, an historical geologist, a biologist interested in the history of animal forms, a philosopher, or a sociologist.

History for the conventional historian involves the narrative[19] and genetic reconstruction of the past by means of the *selection* of a series of sequential, dated events, each of which appears to him to be significantly related to its predecessor and successor; while all, together with those remaining unselected, are regarded as unique, nonrecurrent, and, therefore, insusceptible to that elementary step in the use of scientific method—classification.

Historical reconstruction in geology and paleontology, on the other hand, involves classification from the very start in order to determine the relative ages of fossil forms, strata, and their serial arrangement in a temporal succession, either chronological, or broadly datable. In other words, although the geological sciences, with access to a comparatively small amount of dated or chronologically arrangeable material, have experienced little theoretical difficulty in approaching it armed with scientific method and taxonomic techniques, conventional historians have shied away from a similar treatment of their wealth of dated evidence. Biological history also involves classification. Structurally, it is composed of a series of classified forms, devoid of datable *evidence,* but endowed with temporal *meaning,* which is achieved, first, by converting a present classified array of species in a present order or arrangement from the simple to the complex on the basis of an a priori judgment (often Aristotelian);[20] second,

---

19. "Narrative is . . . a literary form, and its success depends not upon the care with which the details have been investigated, but upon the general ideas by which it is informed, its dramatic construction, and the depiction of character" (Frederick John Teggart, "Anthropology and history," 692). "History is narrative primarily, with optional halts for 'topical' discussion" (A. L. Kroeber, "History and anthropology in the study of civilizations," 160). "The inner compulsions of writing have ruled the historian. The traditional basis of history has been effective narrative" (*The social sciences in historical study,* 160); "History is once more consciously, almost self-consciously, allying itself with literature. Clio has prevailed over Ranke, and we are no longer ashamed of the personal angle or the purple patch" (Vivian H. Galbraith, *An introduction to the study of history,* 75). See also Richard G. Ely, "Mandelbaum on historical narrative: a discussion," 275–94.

20. "Aristotle did not assume the existence of hierarchies. [But] there are many passages in his works which can be made the foundation of an hierarchical universe." The word "hierarchy" does not occur in classical Greek. It appears first in the Pseudo-Dionysius. "The logical hierarchy as we know it comes to us as a series of classes and classes of classes according to which individuals.are grouped into species, species into genera, genera into groups of genera, continuing until one reaches what is believed to be the all-inclusive class. In modern biology we find this sort of thing exemplified on a less than cosmic scale in the Kingdoms, Phyla, Classes, Orders, Families, Genera, Species, and Sub-species" (George Boas, "Some assumptions of Aristotle," 84–85).

by converting that present arrangement from the simple to the complex into a temporal series on the basis of an a priori envisagement of biological change as natural, developmental, progressive, or evolutionary. To many students of culture or society, history is better known in its philosophical than its narrative form, and thus conforms very closely, insofar as principles of organization are concerned, to "history" for the biologist.[21] That is to say, the earliest part of the whole cultural series is achieved, first, by a logical arrangement of existing, undated, or preliterate cultures in an order from the simple to the complex, followed by the continued construction of the cultural series by means of the choice of cultural periods (usually civilizations) withdrawn from the datable histories of datable societies or inhabited areas, and their arrangement in chronological order. The assumption here is that this social series exhibits the total course of cultural change from primitive to civilized man, just as the biological series recapitulates the course of organic change. The total course of cultural change is viewed hypothetically and traditionally, as is biological change, as natural, developmental, progressive, or evolutionary.[22]

It is notable that although the anthropologist regards himself as a scientist and takes pride in that status, the conventional historian, the historian who writes histories of England or France or Mexico, who selects a series of dated events to account for some selected contemporary or antecedent present and embodies it in a narrative structure, is of a different mind. He neither considers himself to be a scientist, desires to be a scientist, or abetted by philosophers who remorselessly analyze "history," deems it possible to become a scientist. True, according to the manuals on historiography, the techniques employed by historians to test the authenticity of documents

21. This, of course, does not include the diffusionist who derives his successions of cultures or culture traits from the study of their geographical positions in a mapped diffusion, aided by assumptions, often borrowed from the age-and-area theory which, in turn is based on botany and zoology.

22. Teggart, *Theory and processes*, 77-151; Bock, *Acceptance of histories*, passim; Hodgen, *Early anthropology*, 431-511. The temporalization "of the chain of being . . . was quite compatible with the idea of fixed species. All that the doctrine of continuous creation in time implied was that nature was not a finished, perfect product once created by God. . . . Once the Aristotelian theory of the fixity of species was abandoned, the way was prepared for the concept of the evolution of forms in accordance with the principle of a hierarchical continuum" (David Bidney, *Theoretical anthropology*, 43-44). "The word science already covers so many different branches of knowledge, employing so many different methods and techniques, that the onus seems to rest on those who seek to exclude history rather than on those who seek to include it. It is significant that the arguments for exclusion come not from scientists . . . but from historians and philosophers anxious to vindicate the status of history as a branch of humane letters. . . . They are so busy telling us that history is not a science . . . *that they have no time for its achievements and potentialities*" (Italics added. Edward Hallet Carr, *What is history?* 78-80).

and dates, or to arrange and file dated materials to be used in "writing" history, are usually designated as scientific[23] in some sense. True, also, historians often make use of conclusions reached in other disciplines by the use of scientific method. They borrow from psychology to motivate their casts of characters and to make their narratives march. Or, assuming that existing preliterate cultures have remained unchanged during long reaches of past time, they borrow from recent anthropologists' descriptions of contemporary "savage" activities to flesh out their own narratives of an earliest historical period. But meanwhile nearly all maintain with vehemence that if scientific method—the morphological, descriptive, and classificatory procedures of the anthropologist—were ever to be employed on dated materials (which are often cultural in character), the result might be something, but it would *not* be "history."[24] For these reasons the anthropological study of the historical cultures, existing and in past time, has been all but foreclosed.

In an effort to obtain further insight into the methodological position or the paradigm of the historian, and hence arrive at some understanding of the provocative rift[25] which cleaves the study of the one creature, man, into two parts, it will be helpful to recall two facts. The first is that history, like anthropology, deals with but a fraction of humanity, an important fraction but nevertheless a fraction. This fractional segment has acquired significance for inquiry because it offers a dated or recorded past; it has usually called Europe or Eurasia its homeland;[26] and it usually has some collective remembrance of experience with, or aspiration for, post-tribal life in political society. Secondly, in a voluminous literature, which rests upon the authority of generations of philosophers and logicians, this cleavage between human history, as the study of the unique, and science as the study of the classifiable,[27] similar, or recurrent, is a source of satisfaction—desirable, self-evident,

23. Charles V. Langlois and Charles Seignobos, *Introduction to the study of history,* 211 ff. "That history can be regarded as a social science needs little argument. . . . For some generations . . . the practice . . . of historians has reflected the scientific spirit" (*The social sciences in historical study,* 18, 21, 26, 30, 86-87, 128, 131-38, 143. Teggart, *Theory and processes,* 5-7, 13, 29, 56, 63, 108.

24. "History would not be itself if it deserted the literary and discursive mold in which its original practitioners cast it" (Henry Stuart Hughes, "The historians and the social scientists," 35).

25. This is the subject of the Social Science Research Council's Bulletin, 64 (1964) entitled *The social sciences in historical study.*

26. Since World War II the historians' interest in African, Asian, South American, or other non-European areas has been expanded.

27. The very idea that historical inquiry might include an interest in "a class of phenomena is certainly calculated to set on edge the teeth of any historian, even of a broadminded institutional historian" (Alfred Louis Kroeber, "History and evolution," 5).

and axiomatic.[28] Indeed, in recent numbers of historical journals one occasionally reads statements which rejoice that an earlier, misguided effort in the nineteenth and early twentieth centuries to reconcile history and scientific method has at last been suppressed by more "rational" considerations. There are few historians who recognize their inquiries as only *one* form of organized interest in the past, who realize that students in other fields also confront historical problems, or who therefore accept the possibility that an interest in historiography might be appropriate among anthropologists, archaeologists, geologists, paleontologists, and biologists. On the contrary, there are many who insist that each historian decides in practice what is significant and what is not, aided merely by common sense, and who share the impatience of those who regard courses in historiography as a waste of time.[29]

In illustration of this prevailing point of view among students of the dated history of mankind, it may be useful to call attention to one or two highly regarded and recent papers, chosen somewhat at random: one by an American historian of high repute, the other by a ranking British scholar. In a presidential address read before the American Historical Association in 1933, entitled "Written History as an Act of Faith," the late Charles Austin Beard (1874–1948) stated with the finality of long repetition that "each historian is a product of his age, and that his work reflects the spirit of the time, of the nation, race, group, class, or section." Moreover, he insisted that every writer of history knows that his colleagues have been influenced in the selection and ordering of dated materials,[30] not by the rigorous usage of scientific method, but by their biases, prejudices, beliefs, affections, general upbringing, and experience.[31] Every written history of a town, county, state, nation, race, group, class, idea, or of the wide, wide world "is a selection and arrangement of facts . . . an

28. A short review of some of the arguments used may be found in William Stull Holt, "The idea of scientific history in America," 352-62.
29. For a more thoughtful analysis of the relation of history to the other social studies, and of its purpose in the study of cultural change, see Leonard Kreiger, "The horizons of history," 62-74.
30. "Empirical data were teaching me that though the available data were potential raw material for the historian . . . it did not by itself constitute history . . . historical facts were statements or affirmations that certain events had taken place which I had the option to use or not use. There was no hard irreducible cluster that had to be taken in toto. I could exercise a discretionary selection . . . historical facts . . . did not take on significance . . . until by using them, I made them come to life" (Leo Gershoy, "Some problems of a working historian," 62).
31. "History is the narrative statement of happenings in the past. No annalist, and no historian attempts to set down all that has taken place. . . . Historical narrative, then, represents only a selection from what is known to have taken place. The contemporary historian . . . presents only such matters, as from his point of view, are of importance" (Teggart, *Theory and processes of history*, 18-19). For an opposing view, see Maurice Mandelbaum, "A note on history as narrative" 13-19.

act of choice," on the part of the historian. Events "are selected and ordered by him as he thinks."[32] The historian who writes history "performs an act of faith. Certainty, as to order and movement, is denied him. . . . His faith is at bottom a conviction that something true can be known about the movement of history, and his decision is a subjective decision, not purely objective discovery." Unaware of, or inattentive to, the fact that geology and paleontology are also in part historical subjects in which inquirers strive to construct chronologies of strata or fossil organisms, give them dates, and seek in this context for uniform processes of geological change, Beard relegates scientific method in relation to the dated events of the human history to a subordinate role, if it is not cast out entirely. Granted that it may be employed "in obtaining accurate knowledge of historical facts, personalities, and movements," and that it enjoys an elevated place "in the hierarchy of values indispensable to the life of a democracy," the occurrences of human history are nevertheless held to be different from the data of physics and other natural sciences "and hence in their totality are *beyond the reach* of that necessary instrument of natural science—mathematics."[33]

Isaiah Berlin's more recent paper entitled "History and theory: the concept of scientific history," and published in 1960 as the leading article in the inaugural number of the periodical, *History and Theory,* strikes the same note. "The purpose of history is to paint a portrait of a situation or a process, which, like all portraits, seeks to capture the unique . . . not to be an X ray which eliminates all but what a great many subjects have in common."[34] Bias is thus enthusiastically embraced. The historical sense "concentrated in an interest in particular events . . . is sharpened by love, hate, or danger." It is quite unlike the objectivity and neutrality of science. It is this very subjectivism which guides the historian in understanding, discovering, and explaining. For "history, and other accounts of human life, are . . . akin to art."[35] Its success depends "on skill in describing, on style,

32. "An extraordinary significance is attached to the fact that every historical explanation involves a three-fold selection—a selection of a theme or problem to be explained, the selection of data considered relevant to the theme or problem, and the selection of an explanatory hypothesis or interpretation" (Sidney Hook, "Objectivity and reconstruction in history," 254).

33. Beard, "Written history."

34. Isaiah Berlin, "History and theory: the concept of scientific history."

35. Historians often try to enjoy the best of two worlds. While claiming that their manner of investigation is scientific, their narrative presentation belongs to the realm of art (Hughes, "The historians and the social scientists," 20–46). Or as John Dewey has said: "The formation of historical judgment lags behind that of physical judgments . . . because . . . historians have not developed the habit of stating . . . the systematic conceptual structures which they employ in organizing their data . . . (John Dewey, *Logic,* 233; quoted in Helen M. Lynd, "The nature of historical objectivity," 34 n.14).

lucidity, choice of examples, distribution of emphasis, and the like."
Science, on the other hand, concentrates on similarities, as does cultural
anthropology within the range of the primitive cultures. But in other
human affairs, namely, the dated history of the civilized peoples,
"it would be absurd to start in this manner." Historians are not
interested in what commonly or often happens in the dated past of
mankind. They are interested "in precisely that which differentiates
one thing, one person, situation, age, pattern of experience, individual
or collective from another." In writing a history of the French
Revolution, the last thing an historian seeks "to do is to concentrate
on only those characteristics which the French Revolution has in
common with other revolutions, to abstract only common, recurrent
characteristics, to formulate laws."[36] Plainly, as C. S. Lewis once
said of medieval literature, so it appears to be for these twentieth-century historians, Beard and Berlin: "the very words *story* and *history*
[have] not yet been desynonymised."[37]

However, lest readers regard these assertions of the opposition
between historical and scientific method as exceptional or extreme,
let him read similar comments by other historians or philosophers.
According to Carl L. Becker, in an oft-quoted essay published in
1932, history is an "imaginative creation." Our profession belongs
to "that ancient and honorable company of wise men of the tribe,
of bards and story-tellers and minstrels, of soothsayers and priests,
to whom in successive ages has been entrusted the keeping of useful
myths. . . . In the history of history, a myth is a once valid but
now discarded version of the human story, as our *now* valid versions
(italics added) will in due course be relegated to the category of
discarded myth."[38] For Miss Wedgwood the historian can never
establish the truth. He can only grope toward it, "with an intellect
which being furnished in the 20th century, finds it extremely difficult
to understand any other. . . . All the efforts of historical scholarship
are ultimately reduced to a mere matter of human opinion."[39]

In the presence of these illustrative envisagements of historical
procedure, and innumerable similar expressions of opinion both early
and late, the anthropologist has been discouraged from addressing

36. "Comparison is one thing that historians boggle at—and with a sound instinct,
granted their addiction . . . [to the idea of] the distinctness and uniqueness of events
. . . (Kroeber, "Integration of the knowledge of man," 118).
37. Clive Staples Lewis, *The discarded image*, 179.
38. Carl Lotus Becker, *Everyman his own historian*, 243, 247.
39. Cicely Veronica Wedgwood, "History and the imagination," 101-102. See also
Carr's candid statement of how he goes to work to "write" history, in *What is history?*
22-23.

anthropological questions to the materials descriptive of the dated historical cultures. To do so would be tantamount to the surrender of his morphological, classificatory, and scientific interests. Not only do historians regard the study of dated materials as their province, but also they regard their use of them in narration as an art, not a science. Instructed by philosophers, the dated events in the narrative series, and, indeed, the totality of recorded events from which these are chosen, are thought to be resistant, as accidental and nonrecurrent, to the classificatory procedures of anthropology or science in general. Of course, as we are reminded by the philosopher, Patrick Gardiner, "it is . . . open to anybody to say that history should strive to become more scientific, that it should seek more precise correlations within its material than those with which it has been satisfied up to now. But when making such recommendations, we must beware of prescribing that history should become other than what it is: for then like Alice in Wonderland, we may find that the baby in our arms has turned into a pig."[40] For this reason, he continues, "there is something fishy about asking the historian questions of the type we should be felt justified in asking a theoretical or practical scientist."[41]

40. For a different point of view, see J. Ambrose Raftis, "Marc Bloch's comparative method and the rural history of medieval England," 349-65.
41. Patrick Gardiner, *The nature of historical explanation*, 53-63.

CHAPTER 2

The Anthropologist and His Use of History

Complexities arise as soon as it becomes necessary to inform oneself concerning the anthropologist's reactions to the assumptions and results of the narrative historian, to other forms of historical reconstruction, or to his own treatment of cultural change as a process in historical time. Although it has been authoritatively declared that "unless the ethnologist defines clearly his concept of history . . . there can be little prospect of arriving at . . . a coherent ethnological theory,"[1] it seems to be true that few students of the preliterate peoples have found it necessary to acquire a firm grasp upon the procedural differences among the traditional, dated, and narrative reconstruction of the past; the chronological reconstruction as it appears in natural sciences, such as historical geology; and that philosophical arrangement of materials in a purported temporal order often referred to as culture history, cultural development or evolution. Indeed, according to Professor Bidney, "with the exception of Kroeber, hardly any anthropologists have ventured to define what they meant by history and the relation of history to a science of ethnology."[2] To most anthropologists, as to many other students, all types of reconstruction of the past are "history." Neither the procedure of the narrative or literary historian, nor that of the philosopher of history, the historical geologist, paleontologist, or biologist has been made the subject of realistic, discriminating, down-to-earth analysis and comparison. If, as seems to be true, the narrative historian, as a user of dated materials, has been unwilling to imagine a possible historical procedure other

1. David Bidney, *Theoretical anthropology,* 280.
2. Ibid., 280. But note that while this philosopher chides the ethnologist for not making clear "his concept of history" he does not require clarity of himself about all other concepts of history in daily use.

than his own, so too the anthropologist has been less than active in acquiring a knowledge of what makes an historian an historian.[3]

As a consequence, many anthropologists are confused. That type of historical inquiry which attempts to arrive at temporal sequences by appealing to the use of dates, or other chronological indicia, is not clearly distinguished from other types which reconstruct the past by other means. Although archaeologists with their artifacts, like the geologists with their fossils, assert that their temporal arrangements are justified because of their correlations with the facts of stratification or radiocarbon dating, many anthropologists aiming at descriptions of the process or processes of change going on in past time look for no such dated sanctions. Only too often that which happens in the observable cultural present is taken to be a replication of what has happened in the past; and there is no demand for an examination of the records of the past to verify this precarious intellectual position.

Meanwhile, in the face of the outspoken insistence by historians that only the historically trained can deal with historical problems, there is not a little discussion of "history" in anthropological councils. There are those, namely, some of the ethnohistorians, who frankly accept the principles of narrative historiography. There are others, such as the functionalists both in anthropology and sociology, who advocate the postponement of the study of the dated past until the present is better understood. Still others, notably Professors Kroeber and Evans-Pritchard, find more likenesses than differences between the work of the historian and that of the anthropologist. While at least two important groups of scholars, the diffusionists and the members of the Kulturkreis Schule, maintain that the past may be reconstructed by the manipulation of materials (usually preliterate and undated) which, apart from their traditional assumptions, concerning cultural change, reflect only present conditions.[4]

Among recent anthropologists who deal almost exclusively with the cultures of primitive peoples, but at the same time express opinions concerning the discipline of "history" are Professor George Peter Murdock and the ethnohistorians. Holding that "the processes by which culture changes are by now reasonably well known to science,"

3. "Though concerned with colonialism, 'westernization,' and kindred topics, the anthropologist . . . has indicated little interest in handling the complex data of documented historical periods, which require insights and methodologies different from those characteristic of ethnological or archeological reconstructions of history" (John William Bennett and Kurt Heinrich Wolff, "Towards communication between sociology and anthropology," 338).
4. For the discussion of the "recovery" of the past by means of the observation of selected present processes, see pp. 15, 17, 18-19, 21, 23, 34, 40, 70.

and preoccupied with the collection of a sample of preliterate materials to the end of achieving fruitful trait classification and comparison, Murdock has been known to describe dated events in two ways—either as unique and unclassifiable or as exhibiting resemblances. "Culture history," he has said in a description of his cross-cultural survey, "is a succession of unique events"; that events "which affect later ones in the same historical sequence are often, if not usually, accidental . . . constantly exerting a disturbing influence."[5] It does not seem to have occurred to Murdock, as he thus subscribes to the narrative historian's view of events, that even though thought of as "disturbances," events might also be subject to classification, both in themselves and in the nature of their effects upon the cultures they disturb.[6] However, to add to the confusion, he has also said that events specifically with respect to time and place, "may resemble one another . . . and exert parallel influences in different cultures." It is thus "possible to view changes in culture . . . in relation to comparable events."[7]

Another effort to reconcile anthropology and history, now enjoying some popularity, is to be found in the work of the *ethnohistorians*. Unhappily the procedure of those who have adopted that appellation is not always the same nor is it easy to describe in a few words. Like the word *history* itself, *ethnohistory* carries a load of variant meanings,[8] and exhibits in practice a diversity of methods and results. After attempting to organize the literature for discussion, one can only say that the term seems to refer usually to one or the other of two types of inquiry, each focused upon the preliterate peoples

5. George Peter Murdock, "The cross-cultural survey," 52.
6. Murdock's method is taxonomic and quantitative. He proposes to deal with a sample in which cultures "will be chosen in equal numbers from all continents and all culture areas, including a representative selection of historical and modern civilizations" (55). His position on the historical cultures may be further illuminated by the following: "in sheer bulk, the mass of descriptive material of interest to the anthropologist probably exceeds by several times that of all the rest of the social sciences put together. . . . Other social scientists concern themselves in the main only with the complex societies of the present and the historical past—perhaps a hundred all told. Anthropologists share their interest in these higher civilizations but also have an equal concern with the many simpler societies of the world, which probably number about three thousand" (George Peter Murdock, "The processing of anthropological materials," 265).
7. George Peter Murdock, "How culture changes," 250.
8. This is made apparent by Bidney in his *Theoretical anthropology* (208, 274-79, 319). Here the term is used to refer to Freud's correlation of dreams with mythological narratives, as a covering term for various types of "historical" interests expressed from Boas to Herskovits, and to procedures in Sir Henry Maine's *Ancient Law*. Compare this with Frederick John Teggart's more orderly analysis in his *Theory and processes of history*, and with remarks made by William Duncan Strong, "Anthropological theory and archeological fact," 364-65, 367.

but differing widely in attitude toward the need for the use of dated documentation.

In what may be called the first or most common type of this anthropological endeavor, the propriety of the use of the word *history* is at best doubtful. It is used by those who are interested primarily in the cultural needs of the so-called developing countries, induced changes, or westernization. Their work is thus more often concerned with recording on-going and current innovations than with the assembly of the chronological or dated events of changes in the past. In short, insofar as they are historians at all, they rely on an implicit doctrine of cultural uniformitarianism, or the purported likeness of present processes of change to past processes. Concerned with "purposive" innovations, or "applied anthropology," they assume, with a certain lack of historical sensitivity, that past processes are elicited when present processes are described.[9]

A prime example of the implied use of the latter doctrine, though there have been many others,[10] is to be found in a United Nations publication, edited by Margaret Mead, entitled *Cultural Patterns and Technical Change.* Since this study was intended for administrative use (or to be put into the hands of "experts, policy makers, specialists, technicians of all sorts, chiefs of missions and teams, members of ministries of health, education, agriculture, and industrial development"),[11] its authors are interested in how certain technical improvements known to western culture may be introduced among "undeveloped" peoples. The emphasis is therefore upon "directed" diffusion, the means for facilitating the acceptability of proffered innovations, or of inducing "harmonious change." In plan and as a manual, Part I presents several informative descriptions of existing cultures: the Burmese, the modern Greeks, the Tiv, the Palau, and the Spanish Americans of New Mexico. Part II considers the fate of certain instances of proffered innovations, those tried and found wanting, and those found acceptable. Most of this however is in the nature of general comment rather than the statement of the results of carefully

9. According to Raymond Firth, the perception of trends of change in social forms by this procedure "has been difficult and subject to considerable error. Partly to meet such problems . . . some social anthropologists have returned after a considerable period of years to the societies they formerly studied. A variant procedure has been for a different social anthropologist to make a restudy of a community investigated earlier." This "replication analysis" is said to have yielded valuable data on the pace of social change in preliterate societies over relatively short periods of the past. ("Social anthropology," I, 323; Walter Goldschmidt, "The anthropological study of modern society," I, 330–39.

10. *Cultural patterns and technical change.* See also for similar examples Felix Maxwell Keesing, *Culture change.*

11. *Cultural patterns,* 16. See also Lucy Mair, "Applied anthropology," I, 325–29.

organized investigations of cultural changes in past time.[12]

Of the Burmese culture, for example, it is said that innovation is an "inherent principle," but acting only in the life of the individual, "not in terms of relationships." From the outset western contact with this area has "cut at the very roots of the traditional, pre-established order, by bringing change where the individual has depended upon immutability."[13] On the other hand, the modern Greek peasant presents obstacles to technical changes. Having accustomed himself to coping with inconveniences, anything that still works can always be patched up and still used, without the irritation attendant upon the adoption of the new. The administrator desiring to introduce innovation in this land has thus had "to point out the mote in the peasant's eye," realizing meanwhile "that the eye is actually adjusted to the mote."[14] Although the Tiv in Nigeria appear to favor innovation, few technical changes have been effected. To be accepted they must be "harmonious with the original culture pattern." In other words, the authors of the manual, after recounting many inexplicable or disappointing experiences in "purposive" change, or "directed" diffusion, agree that innovations may best be introduced, "not through centralized planning, but after the study of local needs."[15]

Their position as ethnohistorians has been analyzed by John Herman Randall Jr. in his *Nature and historical experience* (1958). "The focus in the present of any history," he points out, "first selects *its* past, and designates the particular historical changes that brought about its present state. These changes are then themselves explained by drawing upon the best science of changes in that 'present' . . . a science . . . in which certain patterns of constant operations of human behavior have been arrived at by experimental analysis of observed behavior." Thus, "it is in terms of our present science of human

12. The meagerness of the evidence regarded as acceptable, and the absence of interest in past periods of technical changes which are known to have occurred among at least some of these peoples, may be observed in the fact that conclusions concerning the Burmese were drawn from the writings of British officers of administration, and two studies of Burmese personality "made during the last eight years," together with the personal observation of one individual in one village (*Cultural patterns*, 23, n.3). For the Greeks, information came "from interviews, correspondence, and memoranda" obtained during the one year of 1950-51, and similar sources (Ibid., 57, n.1). Information on the Tiv people came from the accounts of two British administrators plus "a history" of Tiv society by one member of the tribe (Ibid., 96, n.1). The study of the people of Palau is based upon observations made on three trips to the islands in 1944 (Ibid., 126, n.1), while that of the Spanish Americans is based largely on unpublished materials. The published materials came from the U.S. Department of Agriculture (Ibid., 151, n.1).
13. Ibid., 56-57.
14. Ibid., 90-91.
15. Ibid., 122.

behavior, of our psychology, anthropology and social sciences in general, *such as they are* (italics added), that we must ultimately understand past human behavior, if we are to understand it at all."[16] (A prospect which leaves out completely all that dated history might tell us concerning the facts of social changes in the past.)

In two other examples of this type of ethnohistory the assumed adequacy of the use of the description of present processes for obtaining insight into those operating in the past (or the doctrine of uniformity), is made even more explicit. The first to be noted appears in a paper by Murdock.[17] Writing in 1956, he is more than sanguine concerning the knowledge possessed by contemporary anthropologists with respect to existing processes of cultural change, and hence with those operative in the historical past. These existing processes, he says, are not only well known but begin with *innovation*, followed by *social acceptance, selective elimination and integration* (italics added). Innovation, or the formation of a new habit by an individual is subsequently extended to other members of his society. When an innovation is thus extended to another situational context, it becomes a *variation*; while *borrowing* is a common form of innovation dependent upon contact and frequently referred to as *diffusion*.

All of this is accompanied with illustrations drawn from the observation of *existing* preliterate or advanced societies, and from occasional historical sources. But there is no realization whatsoever that in scientific inquiry illustration is *not* enough; that the processes of cultural change are *not* well known; or that change, since it takes place in time, can best be studied with an eye to the dated records of the cultural past. Essentially what is involved in Professor Murdock's argument is the advocacy of the extrapolation of descriptions of present cultural changes upon past cultural phenomena. But as Professor George Boas has said of this infatuation with the present, "the present is an extremely slippery creature . . . no sooner grasped than it becomes the past . . . Probably nothing has been done more to falsify our knowledge of our fellow men"[18] than to select one era of human history as identical with those which have preceded it. It cannot be assumed with safety that the dated events of cultural changes in the past, so far scarcely noticed, will accord with those taking place in any selected "present."

A second influential example of the use of this same type of paradigm,

16. John Herman Randall, Jr., *Nature and the historical experience*, 61–62.
17. Murdock, "How culture changes," 247–60.
18. George Boas, "The living book," 1972–1975.

and burdened with all of its faults, appears in the book called
Innovation: The Basis of Cultural Change, by Homer Garner Barnett.
According to an editor's preface, the book was written in the first
place because studies of cultural diffusion, though long continued,
had been judged to have failed to produce a new theory of the innovative
process; and, secondly, because "we simply do not know . . . whether
any or all the various trends in organizational development—themselves
often innovations—will foster or discourage the innovative process."[19]
The argument is thus oriented toward "the possible consequences
to science and science-based technology of . . . the constant expansion
of governmental functions," some of which are expressed with
reference to induced innovations in the undeveloped countries. Professor Barnett's objectives are therefore not unlike the administrative
preoccupations of the compilers of the United Nations study, and
his interest in the *dated* study of past changes is equally minimal.

In order to confer "universal validity" upon his conclusions,
"regardless of where changes occur," Professor Barnett chooses to
base them (somewhat remotely) upon the examination of a sample
of cultures; and moreover on a sample of only six sources of
"empirical" data accumulated since 1938 (or during the fifteen-year
period before the book's publication in 1953). This sample, "selected
for expediency,"[20] is composed of "the total cultures of five ethnic
groups:" the American, which "understandably contributed the most";
three Indian tribes in the Western United States; the Palauans of
Micronesia; and an Indian Shaker cult. It is impossible to form a
judgment of how long the investigations of any of these groups were
carried on, by whom, or in response to what questions.[21] However,

19. Homer Garner Barnett, *Innovation,* vi–vii.
20. Ibid., 2.
21. As for the three Indian tribes—the Yurok, the Tsimshian, and the Yakima—there
is no evidence that innovations among them were either prolonged or profound. His
study of cultural changes among the Yurok took place in 1938. First contact with
the tribe is said to have begun in 1850. Beyond this, no documentation, dates, or
other forms of historical evidence are vouchsafed. The Tsimshian, in British Columbia,
were visited by investigators in 1940. Historical information is limited to the inference
that "their contacts with European traders" began in the 1830s. No more is offered
concerning the *dated* history of innovations among the Yakimas. They are said to
have occupied a reservation in south central Washington since the 1850s. They were
"investigated" in 1942. The Palauans of Micronesia, who are said to have had "rather
continuous contact with Europeans and Asiatics since the 18th century," were "studied"
over a period of nine months in 1947–48. It is stated that the Indian Shaker cult
was established in New York in 1774, and also noted that "history" affords material
for the study of their religious practices over a 60-year period. "But no attempt has
been made to cover the literature systematically." Beyond these meager temporal
notations, and although the cultural innovations which interest him have taken place
in past time, Professor Barnett's work is innocent of historical or dated information
(Ibid., 2–7).

the degree of the author's interest in historical records may be inferred from his statement that "application of historical perspective, and the urge to link events in a temporal series, is not a pronounced trait in most societies. . . . History as such . . . is beyond their purview . . . Discrete events are not aligned on a scale of past and present in a way to induce the concept of change."[22] Barnett also concedes that no attempt was made to cover the literature systematically or to correlate the interpretations of different observers.[23] Rather it is his intention, with the slender evidence indicated, "to formulate a general theory of the nature of innovation . . . the appearance of novel ideas . . . the factors that influence their acceptance or rejection," stopping short of an interest in time relationships, location and quantity.[24] Though he states in one place that "what is needed are answers to the questions of why, which, when, and how, . . . and within what limits . . . certain traits and not others are added or subtracted, or fused with others,"[25] his approach is neither historical nor statistical.[26] The basic innovative processes, or the sought-for processes of cultural change, are derived, not from the study of recorded and dated human experience, and not even from a wide array of descriptive primitive materials, but from Barnett's personal analysis conducted in the on-going present or recent past. The processes referred to are present processes to which, so far as we can judge, he alone had access; and are expressed in simple declarative sentences. Extrapolation from the present on a frankly unexamined past is taken for granted as sound practice.

Another school of ethnohistorians, perhaps ethnohistory proper, differs sharply in purpose and procedure from those who have merely assumed the title on the basis of recovering the preliterate past by extrapolation from the preliterate present. These other ethnohistorians, indeed, take their fellows to task for lacking a true understanding of history, and for plunging into "the limbo of inference" characteristic of many studies of diffusion.[27] They take issue not only with the common assumption that the pasts of all preliterate peoples are either

22. Ibid., 62.
23. Ibid., 7.
24. Ibid., 1.
25. Ibid., 11.
26. Ibid., 1.
27. It has been said, not without cause, that the main reason why ethnology "has matured so slowly as an historical science is the long-standing preoccupation with diffusional studies and the neglect of direct history" (William Nelson Fenton, "The training of historical ethnologists in America," 328. See also William Nelson Fenton, "Fieldwork, museum studies, and ethnohistorical research," and William C. Sturtevant, "Anthropology, history, and ethnohistory."

irrecoverable, or recoverable only by use of the age-and-area theory or similar devices described by Sapir, but also with the employment of descriptions of the preliterate present as though it were necessarily a replication of the preliterate past.

They point out, on the contrary, that the histories of a goodly number of primitive peoples may be recovered for several centuries with documentary assistance. Consequently, while dedicating themselves to the historical studies of such peoples, they chide the conventional historian, long absorbed solely in the historical fate of European man, with neglecting these important archival resources.[28] Though earlier examples of their work date back to the turn of the century or a little later,[29] the periodical, *Ethnohistory*, only began publication in 1954, preceded and followed by important papers on the subject by Professor William N. Fenton and others.[30]

It must be regarded as significant, however, that none of the earlier ethnohistorians of this type, nor those who have come later, have found reason to fault the procedures of their colleagues in departments of history or to question the assumption of the uniqueness and unclassifiability of events, the selection and serial arrangement of events, or the adoption of a narrative style of presentation. Insofar as their use of dated ethnic material is concerned they have remained conventional historians, and urge those interested in the field to seek instruction from professional narrative historiographers.[31] They have not taken steps to carry the old anthropological problem of cultural change into the domain of datable history by the collection and classification of the recorded events of changes among the preliterate peoples who possess dated records. Although scientists by allegiance and tradition, they have accepted without comment the lineal, literary form imparted to the recovery of the human past by the practicing historiographer and the assumed impossibility of the employment of dated events in anything but a narrative structure. Their work, usually

28. "Professional historians report that interest in the American Indians is discouraged . . . in the present day training of American historians. . . . But if there are few ethnologically minded historians there are also equally few historically minded ethnologists. . . . Documentary study of American Indian groups has been tolerated, but not actively encouraged" (*Ethnohistory* I: 1-2).
29. Ethnohistory "is neither a modern method nor a modern field of research" (Frederica de Laguna, editor, *Selected papers from the American Anthropologist*, 456).
30. Nancy Oestreich Lurie, "Ethnohistory: an ethnological point of view," 80-81. See also for text and bibliography Bernard S. Cohn, "Ethnohistory."
31. Fenton, "Training of historical ethnologists," 331, 334, 338. See this important paper for a more detailed description of procedures and sources. "The ethnohistorical method is distilled from concepts arrived at in working with living cultures in the field. . . . The model of my concept of ethnohistory is field-oriented, having reciprocal lines running to the museum on the one hand, and to the library and archive on the other" (Fenton, "Fieldwork," 75).

restricted to tribal subject-matter, drawn from both field and archive, is thus indistinguishable from that of the conventional historian.

In addition to the misapprehensions of those anthropologists who adhere to the concept of the uniqueness and unclassifiability of events, to the acceptability of the extrapolation of presently observed "processes" upon the unknown past, and to the narrative presentation of dated preliterate documentary materials, the confusion between anthropology and history is aggravated by the activities and pronouncements of those who call themselves *functionalists*. These students profess either a lack of interest in the temporal aspects of culture, preliterate or advanced, or prefer to postpone any historical effort until such time as the rapidly disappearing "savage" shall have been adequately analyzed and described in his existing condition. Their emphasis is therefore upon the description of internal cultural processes presently operative in preliterate group life.[32]

In an article entitled "Should anthropologists be historians?" Professor Schapera says:

The historian, if one may judge by what professional historians themselves say, is interested primarily in human affairs, and the activities of the *past*. . . . The anthropologist, so long as field work continues to be considered an essential part of his personal research activity, must of necessity be concerned with mainly the *present*, with the description . . . of social institutions as they occur *nowadays* . . . His understanding will admittedly be more complete if he can learn not only how they function but also how they developed. But he seeks knowledge of the past for the specific, if not sole purpose of illuminating the present . . . (Italics added).[33]

The functionalists, not unlike the sociologists with respect to western or advanced societies, seek to give primary attention to ways of eliciting the general "laws" of social systems, restricting themselves to the study of preliterate societies as they exist in the present.[34] In taking this position, "the functional or organismic theory of society," according to Evans-Pritchard, "is not new. . . . What is new is the insistence that a society can be understood satisfactorily without

---

32. The reader in search of greater clarity will do well to examine the differing opinions of the concept of "function." See, for example, Raymond Firth, "Function," 237-55, and also Kenneth E. Bock, "Evolution, function, and change," 229-37.

33. Isaac Schapera, "Should anthropologists be historians?" 153.

34. ". . . they have totally rejected the reconstruction from circumstantial evidences of the history of primitive peoples for whose past documents and monuments are totally, or almost totally, lacking." In addition, some, notably Malinowski say "that even when the history of a society is recorded it is irrelevant to a functional study of it" (Edward Evan Evans-Pritchard, "Social anthropology: past and present," 21).

reference to its past."[35] Since the functionalist seeks to exclude the recorded phenomena of the human past, or of recorded cultural changes, in order to free his hands for the study of presently operating, internal cultural processes, he not only avoids the confusions incident to an effort to recover the patterns of the dated past, he also holds aloof from diffusionist efforts at historical reconstruction and from all others purporting to reconcile anthropology and history.

Unfortunately, other anthropologists have not been quite so prudent. Indeed, there is a somewhat ambivalent group whose members try to conduct their inquiries in at least two roles, that of the historian and that of the descriptive scientist, but still without coming cleanly to grips with the differences between descriptive, historical, and scientific procedures, and especially without the benefit of a careful analysis of the differences which prevail among the several types of historical reconstruction.

Professor Kroeber's writings on anthropology and history are an example of the resulting ambiguity. His amazing, and frequently quoted, assertion that history and anthropology are more alike than different,[36] together with the inference that students of historyless peoples have therefore been historians all along, is a case in point.

The reliability or unreliability of this judgment rests upon three prior intellectual positions: first, on the mental suppression of the primary and significant differences between the two disciplines, namely, their respective accessibility or inaccessibility to dated documentation; secondly, on an overemphasis on the use in both anthropology and history of cultural description; and thirdly, on a frequent disregard of the incontestable association of change and the historical enterprise with the passage of time.[37]

In a paper entitled *"History and science in anthropology"* published in 1935, and in a later group of reprinted papers, entitled *An anthropologist looks at history* (1963), Kroeber witnesses firmly to the central importance in the study of man of historical investigation, together with an acknowledgment of the historiographical shortcomings of an anthropology restricted to the study of preliterate, dateless peoples.

---

35. Ibid., 18–19. See also Clyde Kluckhohn, "Anthropology in the 20th century," 756. The procedure may have been encouraged by administrative efforts to govern or assist the undeveloped peoples.

36. See Bidney, *Theoretical anthropology*, 252ff, for the philosophical reconciliation of this contradiction, and an account of the adverse response of Franz Boas.

37. "The simplest definition of history is that it is change through time." George Gaylord Simpson, *This view of life,* 121. Consult Simpson on his views of geology, history, and change.

In recent decades, he points out, "there has been an inclination to shift ethnographic studies from Tikopians, Hopi, Nuer, and other non-literates and primitives . . . to communities within literate civilizations. . . . Yet it is plain that face-to-face community studies alone will never suffice for an understanding of a culture as large as that of China, of a nation like the French, or even of a smaller one like the Danes."[38] The whole of a society or culture is "founded in and produced so largely by the past, that an adequate understanding of its present necessarily involves knowledge of its past. [But] to this past, ethnographic primary investigation, being essentially synchronic in its approach, can attain only indirectly and very imperfectly."[39]

On other occasions, however, Professor Kroeber retreats from this acknowledgment of the differences between the dated recovery of the past of a culture, and its present anthropological description. He then makes no distinction between the occasional, episodic, and often piecemeal cultural descriptions sometimes introduced into the dated serial structures of many narrative histories (or the social evolutionary series, for that matter) and the extended descriptive, morphological efforts by anthropologists designed to set forth in inclusive detail the present condition of existing primitives. Disregarding the fact that history (broadly defined) would not be history were it not for the historian's ineluctable commitment to temporal and chronological interests (realized in part by the use of datable materials) and fixing his attention solely on those historians who pause from time to time in their dated narrations to describe the cultural activities of certain human groups at certain dated periods, he goes a step further. He flatly asserts that the distinctive feature of the historical enterprise is *not* that of "dealing with sequences."[40] On the contrary, he envisions the purpose of the historian, like that of the anthropologist, to be the achievement of descriptive interpretations, or "descriptive integrations." He expresses the conviction that "the essence of history is not the time element (sic). . . . Since either space or time may be held constant in a particular history, neither element may be regarded

---

38. Alfred Louis Kroeber, "What ethnography is," 136–37.
39. Alfred Louis Kroeber, "History and science in anthropology," 539–69. See also Bidney, *Theoretical anthropology*, 252–62.
40. ". . . the time element is not the most distinctive factor in history," but superficially assumed. He asserted that the essence "of the process of historical thought" (citing Burckhardt's *Renaissance* and Tacitus' *Germania*) "will continue to fail of being grasped *as long as time is considered most important in that essence*" (Italics added. Alfred Louis Kroeber, "History and evolution," *Southwestern Journal of Anthropology*, 12–13).

as essential. The essential factor is an analytic-synthetic characterizing description.''[41]

Some years later, in 1950 and again in 1961, a similar argument was advanced by the British social anthropologist, Professor Evans-Pritchard. ''The main differences between history and anthropology,'' said he, ''are not aim or method, for fundamentally both are trying to do the same thing.'' The fact that an anthropologist studies people face-to-face and the historian in documents yielding dates ''is a technical not a methodological difference.''[42] Nor does the fact ''that anthropological studies can as a rule be of people only over a short period of time constitute a vital difference. Some historians also cover only a few years.''[43] What descriptive anthropologists have done for existing preliterate, nonhistorical peoples is precisely what descriptive historians have done for early periods of European society—the Merovingian, the Carolingian, Norman, or Anglo-Saxon.[44] Such historians, while in the act of describing these cultural periods, are not concerned immediately with the construction of either a prior or a subsequent dated sequence, though the described period may be an intrinsic part of such a sequence. ''I conclude therefore, following Professor Kroeber, that while there are many differences between social anthropology and historiography they are differences of technique, of emphasis, and of perspective, and not of difference of method and aim.''[45]

These brief comments suggest that neither Kroeber, Evans-Pritchard, nor those others who have subscribed to one or another of their arguments, have felt it necessary to deal in depth with the essential nature of dated historical inquiry; nor with those undated variants based upon doctrines of development, evolution, or progress;

41. For Kroeber's controversy with Franz Boas on this point, see Bidney, *Theoretical anthropology*, 252-54. ''The notion of a 'timeless history' proposed by Kroeber is a contradiction in terms'' Ibid., 280. ''The only specifically historical category is that of time sequence'' (Henry Stuart Hughes, ''The historians and the social scientists,'' 32).
42. Edward Evan Evans-Pritchard, *Anthropology and history*, 14; ''Social anthropology: past and present,'' 23-24.
43. Evans-Pritchard, *Anthropology and history*, 58-59.
44. Ibid., 54.
45. Evans-Pritchard, *''Social anthropology: past and present,''* 25. This view has been shared by others. ''A great deal of historical writing today is concerned less with the succession of events than with enduring relationships. . . . Evans-Pritchard's description of anthropologists as engaged in comparing integrative accounts of primitive peoples at a moment in time . . . is hard to distinguish from Postan's picture of historians 'weaving . . . some historical facts with other historical facts into a cloth of an epoch' '' (Keith Thomas, ''Anthropology and history,'' 5, note 13). See also Henry Stuart Hughes, *History as art and as science;* Philip Bagley, *Culture and history.*

nor with the peculiar intellectual difficulties to be encountered in each.

To be sure, in publishing his *Configurations of Culture Growth* in 1948, Kroeber seems on occasion to have attempted a reassessment of his earlier position. Instead of insisting in this book that "the essence of history is not the time element," he frankly turns to dated materials, adopting as a problem the recurrent appearance at differing dates and places of cultures already classified as "civilizations."[46] While tracing the tantalizing appearances and disappearances of these periods of high achievement he uses as historical or dated indices the productions of datable individuals recognized as superior in philosophy, science, and the arts.[47] Moreover, one of the important questions requiring the use of dates (indicating onset and ending) is that of the temporal duration of this class of cultural periods. In justifying their study by an ethnologist,[48] he describes himself as "an anthropologist dealing with wholly historical data" and, contrary to his earlier position, refers to history and anthropology as "indubitably distinct." However, in later years, and in spite of his venture as an anthropologist into the realm of dated materials, he seemed unable to shake off an initial confusion, or his conception of the historical enterprise articulated earlier. "While history in its popular and most specific sense," he said in 1955, "consists mostly of narrative, this is at times suspended to allow of descriptions of new peoples, of a city, or a condition or period. The *difference* (italics added) between diachronic and synchronic presentation can therefore hardly be cardinal."[49] Still later in 1958 he again declared that dated events were to be regarded as unique and insusceptible to classification, and this in the face of the actual classifications of similar events to be found in the book, *Configurations of Culture Growth*. History, he says, "deals with events with emphasis on uniqueness and change."[50] In 1964, it was reiterated that "historians look for the unique . . . anthropology for such general and recurrent processes

46. See partial history of this problem in Margaret T. Hodgen, *Early anthropology in the sixteenth and seventeenth centuries*, 256, 288, 462-63, 500; also much discussion of relevant matters in Frederick John Teggart, *Theory and processes of history*, especially under the rubric of "progress" in the index.

47. As was no doubt acceptable in a pilot study, much of the raw historical material employed by Professor Kroeber was taken from encyclopedias, not from a wide-ranging study of the relevant historical literatures (Alfred Louis Kroeber, *Configurations of culture growth*, 849).

48. Ibid., 6, 804, 813.

49. Alfred Louis Kroeber, "Integration of the knowledge of man," 110.

50. Ibid., 160.

as may occur in the multifarious events of history, or in the diverse societies, institutions, customs, and beliefs of mankind."[51]

Despite the misapprehensions of those who seek to identify the methods and results of history with those of anthropology, and despite the opposition of functionalists to any exploration of the cultural experiences of the dated peoples, the oldest effort to reconcile the two disciplines is to be found among the diffusionists. The longevity of this form of inquiry is probably derived from an ancient and common-sense recognition of a close relationship between the migrations of peoples and the mingling of their cultures.[52] At all events, diffusionism today is the modern version of an old solution of an old problem of cultural similarities or correspondences. It has persisted in thought certainly from the Renaissance, and long before academic anthropology assumed its present organization and methodological structure. Latterly this solution has been considered as an alternative to another old paradigm of the process of cultural change, or that envisioned logically as natural, inevitable, continuous, developmental, or evolutionary.

At the turn of the century, or during the forty-year period from 1880 to 1920, when the logical, hierarchical, and evolutionary arrangement of cultural changes had come under well-deserved critical scrutiny, attention was redirected[53] to the problem presented by the existence of classes of similar traits in the cultures of primitive peoples, often widely separated in space. These, it came to be assumed on the basis of tradition (and not a little dated evidence of human migrations in the dated period), were ascribable to cultural changes or innovations brought about by human contact or borrowing. But since the geographical distribution of these similarities or correspondences (assumed to be due to contact or borrowing) were unaccompanied in existing descriptions of preliterate cultures with dates—since they were, therefore, unarrangeable chronologically and unexplained by historical records—it became the objective of certain anthropologists to find means to interpret their geographical arrangement chronologically, to interpret them temporally, and thus to that extent, to introduce temporal or "historical investigation into undated anthropological materials."[54]

51. Alfred Louis Kroeber, *Anthropology*, 4.
52. Hodgen, *Early anthropology*, 254–63, 295–349.
53. See the literature of the Boas school of anthropology and the controversy between Boas and Kroeber.
54. For a succinct discussion of distributional analyses applied to nonhistorical peoples but for "historical" purposes, see Fred Eggan, "Social anthropology and the method of controlled comparison," 112–116. In reading this discussion it should be borne

The literature produced by such students is massive. It will suffice at this time to refer only to Edward Sapir's little classic, *Time Perspective in Aboriginal American Culture,* published in 1916, because it deals solely with the methods and techniques employed in temporalizing spatial distributions of similar undatable primitive culture traits.

"Cultural anthropology," says Sapir in the introductory sentence to the book,

is more and more rapidly getting to realize itself as an historical science. Its data cannot be understood, either in themselves or in relation to one another, except as end-points of specific sequences of *events* (italics added) reaching back into the remote past . . . primitive culture consists throughout of phenomena that, so far as the ethnologist is concerned, must be worked out historically, that is in terms of actual happenings, *however inferred,* that are conceived to have a *specific sequence,* a specific localization, and specific relations among themselves. . . . The question immediately suggests itself: how inject a chronology into this confusing mass of purely *descriptive* fact? . . . Is it possible to read time perspective into the flat surface of . . . culture as we read space perspective into the flat surface of a photograph? (Italics added)[55]

Then follows a close analysis of the forms of evidence or inference available to the historically-minded anthropologist, as a student of the nonhistorical peoples. These forms of inference are divided into the *direct* and the *indirect.* As direct evidence Sapir recognizes the importance of historical documentation, such as that to be found in the *Jesuit Relations,* Cook's *Voyages,* native testimony, and stratified archaeological testimony. As for indirect evidence (the main object of his analysis) the list is much longer and the argument much tighter. It includes such subjects as the geographical distribution of similar culture traits and what that distribution may safely imply; the means for determining the relative ages of like culture elements in a distribution; and many other inferential types of documentation of extreme interest and ingenuity. The author concludes his discussion with these words: "A possible conclusion may have been left in the mind of the reader that I attach exaggerated importance to the historical value of purely inferential evidence . . . Such an impression is certainly

in mind that the term "comparative method" may be used in two ways: (1) that involving simple comparison for the discovery of likeness or difference; and (2) that associated with progressionism, developmentalism, or evolutionism and defined by Auguste Comte, after long previous use by others, as the identification of the present or coexisting cultural series with the time of historical series, in order to arrive at an "ideal" series (see Teggart, *Theory and processes,* 102–109, 125; and Kenneth E. Bock, The comparative method of anthropology). See also "Diffusion."

55. Edward Sapir, *Time perspective in aboriginal American culture,* 1–2.

not intended. *I would not dispute for an instant the general superiority of direct (dated) to inferential evidence in the establishment of cultural sequences''* (Italics added). But the handling of historical documentation is held to be relatively obvious. For this, like the ethnohistorians, he sends his readers back to the traditional historical manuals.[56]

Among those diffusionists tacitly included in Sapir's summary analysis of method, but not stressed owing to his Americanist concentration, were the members of the *Kulturkreis Schule.* This group, composed largely of Viennese and German ethnologists, started its work in the 1880s and 1890s. They too were initially concerned with the introduction of temporal depth into the descriptive materials made available by students of existing preliterate and nonhistorical peoples,[57] and with many of the techniques later described by Sapir. But they differed from other students of the same problem in that, once having introduced a time element into such cultures (to their satisfaction), they pushed on still further. They made it their objective to attempt the unification of the historical experience of mankind as a whole by drawing together: (1) the results of inferential, nondocumentary, preliterate "history"; (2) the results of stratified archaeological history; and (3) the seeming likenesses and persistencies of similar traits and ideas as they were revealed in the advanced or civilized cultures by the use of dated documentation. They attempted to combine in a single temporal scheme what they took to be the extreme antiquity of the existing cultural behavior of primitive man[58] with the seemingly

56. Ibid., 86.
57. A pioneer in this movement was said by Father Wilhelm Schmidt (1868-1954) to be Friedrich Ratzel (1844-1904) who advocated the necessity of research into the distribution of "the actual arts and customs of early (or primitive) civilizations from race to race and land to land," by use of mapping and inferences drawn from the age-and-area hypothesis (Wilhelm Schmidt, "Primitive man," I, 17. See other publications of Father Schmidt: *Der Ursprung der Gottesidee: Eine historisch-kritsche und positiv studie* (1912). See also Clyde Kluckhohn, "Developments in the field of anthropology in the 20th century," 760; "Some reflections on the method and theory of the Kulturkreislehre," 160; Roland B. Dixon, *The building of cultures*, 227-241: and Hermann Baumann, "Fritz Graebner," VI, 240-41.
58. According to Father Schmidt, the first task of investigation will be "to begin with those races as to whose historical age there is *no* doubt, and then, penetrating farther into the past, determine exactly, and on objective evidence, the age of every type we meet with, and by comparing these types . . . establish the actual historical succession of their appearance." Turning then to similarities in cultures, connection amongst them was to be proved by establishing not only contact (by migration) but continuity of contact. Such an historical method enabled the investigator to show these connections in a chronological series, a fact of great importance in the cases of tribes which possess no written documentation. It also permitted discrimination among the diverse forms which result when contact has taken place—the mixed cultures, those involving minor transmissions across cultural borders, or complete fusions. The final step was to establish spheres of likeness and age among peoples who have been in contact, and to derive from them successions antecedent to the appearance of the civilizations (Schmidt, "Primitive man," 10).

like culture elements indicated by the artifacts of prehistoric man, and with the behavior of the several groups of human beings for whose past there exists dated documentation.

The result of the arduous and ingenious study of these three bodies of suggested historical evidence was the disclosure of what these highly qualified and thoughtful investigators regarded as a certain number of universal culture traits or complexes, "core cultures," "spheres," or "persistent aggregates of culture elements appearing (through time) in a fashion too consistent to be fortuitous." According to Professor Kroeber, the German-Austrian School "posits some seven or eight original Kulturkreise."[59] These are not merely geographical spheres of influence, or areas of culture; they are culture types or "blocks of cultural material," dating back in their essence to prehistoric times, and since then diffused by migration over the world.[60] The task of culture history thus became for them "the segregation of any given culture into the elements derived from the several Kulturkreise."[61]

By using typological and chronological procedures, as well as the age and area hypothesis,[62] the founders of the school thus came ultimately to correlate the antiquity, or temporal earliness, of certain primitive traits and cultures with their relative geographical and cultural universality. That is to say, starting with purportedly the most rudimentary (or earliest)[63] peoples in southeastern Australia and in the southern extremity of South America, cultural similarities or

---

59. Alfred Louis Kroeber, "Diffusionism," V, 141.

60. Kluckhohn, "Some reflections on the Kulturkreislehre," 162. "The culture-strata . . . hypothesis . . . attempts to explain the cultures of all the world's people as the result of seven or eight successive and world-wide migrations, setting out from somewhere in Southeastern Asia and the adjacent parts of Oceania, and each carrying with it a supposedly distinct trait-complex. The existing situation is thus accounted for as the result of the super-imposition of these human floods as if they were lava flows" (Dixon, *Building of cultures*, 241).

61. Kroeber, "Diffusionism," 141; Wilhelm Koppers, "Diffusion," 169–79.

62. "One of the more recent exponents of the procedure (Van Bulck in 1932) makes an urgent plea to anchor the *kulturkreis* in every way to the facts established by stratigraphic archeology, physical anthropology, linguistics, and documentary history" (William Duncan Strong, "Historical approach in anthropology," 390).

63. Here, of course, though attempting to be anti-evolutionary in method, these students allowed an ancient hierarchical concept of "inner development" to creep into and condition their thinking (see Schmidt, *The culture historical method*, 11–12, 25, 347 and Hodgen, *Early anthropology*, 396–418; 449; 451–52; 582–84). For a reversal of this position by Wilhelm Koppers, a current member of the school, see Christoph von Fürer-Haimendorf, "Culture history and cultural development," 156: "In a paper read on August 27, 1954, at the Congress of Americanists in São Paulo, . . . Koppers declares himself in favor of an approach to problems of historical connections which starts from the more recent and tangible materials, and then, going backwards, and, so to say, lifting layer after layer, tries to penetrate to the older and finally the oldest common features."

parallels were collected from among museum artifacts and in the descriptive literature. Pressing chronological inferences from similarities still further, other instances of parallels, taken to be ancient and representative of an Urkultur, were searched for in the descriptive literature of other cultures on a wider and wider geographical plan, including not only those of primitive or "earliest" man, but also prehistoric and historical man.

CHAPTER 3

Obstacles to the Use of Dated Events of Cultural Changes by Anthropologists

Now whatever the accomplishments of anthropologists, Kulturkreis theorists, or ethnohistorians in their studies of preliterate man (and they have been many and distinguished), their early and usual withdrawal from the study of human cultures everywhere and at all times—in essence their withdrawal from the study of cultural change by means of the dated record of changes—has meant several things. It has meant, first, the choice for study of a sample of cultures, out of the total array of cultures, past and present, and a somewhat atypical sample at that.[1] For mankind (it cannot be too often repeated) differs essentially from his brethren in the animal world in at least two major characteristics: his responsiveness to change in his behavioral or cultural activities; and his exclusive possession for at least a portion of his residence on the planet, of a dated record of many of such changes.

Anthropology, as now constituted, is not prepared to take the best advantage of these invaluable dated assets. Nonliterate peoples who form, for the most part, the anthropologist's sample, are historyless peoples. As members of a sample, therefore, they are unrepresentative of historical mankind, or mankind as a whole, and unrepresentative in one of the very aspects often said to be his most human.

Secondly, by reason of the dateless condition of the major portion of their sample, most anthropologists have been compelled either to avoid problems falling into a temporal dimension or more bewilder-

---

1. According to Professor Nadel this is a "leftover" sample of "strange," "unfamiliar," "exotic" folk, whose customs are "grotesque and to some extent unintelligible" (Siegfried Ferdinand Nadel, *The foundations of social anthropology*, 1, 6–7); see also Margaret T. Hodgen, "Anthropology, history and science," 282–87.

ingly, to attempt solutions without benefit of dates along avenues of chronological expediency. One of these has been the age-and-area theory in its several forms; another, conjectural history in the form of various progressivisms, developmentalisms, or evolutionisms; while still another has involved a conscious or unconscious appeal to the doctrine of uniformitarianism, borrowed perhaps from botany or geology, two other sciences in historical difficulties.[2] The conscious, or more often unconscious use of this doctrine, which assumes the likeness of past and present processes, has purportedly permitted the recovery of the nonliterate past by the observation of the nonliterate (or even the literate) present. Indeed, the crux of the disunity in the study of the totality of mankind lies in the fact that while historians construct something called "history" out of dated documentation which is hopefully regarded as literary, the anthropologists recover the past, or something called "history" out of materials which (with a few exceptions) have no dates but are nevertheless regarded as the product of the use of scientific method.

Thirdly, the adoption by anthropologists of this historyless segment of mankind, together with the use of undated devices for reconstructing its past, has brought with it the tacit acceptance of a view of events advocated by a single group of students of events, namely, the narrative historians. Though anthropologists regard themselves as scientists, dated events, at the bidding of conventional historiographical thought, are taken to be unique, nonrecurrent, unclassifiable, and insusceptible to the use of scientific method, despite frequent admissions that "history repeats itself." It is clear therefore that had anthropology consulted historical geology as a model of scientific method instead of history or biology the results might have been very different. It is also clear that enlarging the sample at this time to include the historical cultures will entail not only a confrontation of some magnitude between investigators but a temptation to retreat before old obstacles, real or imagined.

Should the anthropologist decide to join the historian in the use of dated in addition to undated cultural materials, the first obstacle encountered will no doubt be an increase in the sheer mass of relevant materials. Already, to some students of the historyless segment of mankind their limited sample seems to possess almost prohibitive dimensions. Although estimates vary, that offered by Hobhouse, Wheeler, and Ginsberg in 1915, and later adopted by Arnold Toynbee

2. "Pseudo historical sequences are most extensively used in historical biology, where historical inference must so often be based on living organisms that are in fact contemporaneous and not sequential" (Simpson, *This view of life*, 142).

in his *Study of History,* placed the number of primitive peoples at 650.[3] Another by James G. Leyburn reached the sum of "over 12,000 tribes, language groups, nations, clans, and other social divisions."[4] The most recent, that of Professor George P. Murdock, claims a total of more than 3,000.[5] But of these, he says, "the descriptive data of no other social science can even remotely compare in quantity with the wealth of ethnographic detail available on these thousands of peoples. For a comparable situation one must turn to such biological sciences as botany and zoology."

However that may be, a measure of composure is attainable. For, if one turns to the biological sciences, the sum of the historical peoples, large as it is, added to that of the nonhistorical peoples, is still far less than that confronted by the naturalist. Over the years, the exercise of taxonomic activity in biology and paleontology has led to vast stores of organized data. We are told that the number of species of living animals is set at no less than one million, a sum which excludes all species of living plants, and all extinct forms.[6] In other words, the total number of groups or classes of interest to naturalists, is not like that said to confront the anthropologist, a mere 3,000. It may well exceed the total of all primitive and advanced cultures past and present, living today or long forgotten. Nevertheless this obstacle of size has been surmountable.

It should also relieve anxiety concerning the wisdom of addressing anthropological questions to dated materials to realize that another obstacle set up by passionate defenders of orthodox historiographical theory, such as Beard, Berlin, and Becker, has already attracted opposition. In several walks of academic life there are those who openly scoff at the ancient doctrine of the uniqueness of events. It has been called "a paralyzing platitude"; and in a recent volume entitled *What is History?* Edward Hallett Carr asserts that "the very use of language commits

the historian like the scientist to generalization. The Peloponnesian War and the Second World War were very different, and both were unique. But the historian calls them both wars. . . . When Gibbon wrote of both the

3. Or that part of a total about which the authors "happened to find information that was sufficiently full and sufficiently trustworthy for their purposes" (Leonard Trelawney Hobhouse, Gerald Clair Wheeler, and Morris Ginsberg, *The material culture and social institutions of the simpler peoples*).
4. James Graham Leyburn, *Handbook of ethnography,* v.
5. George P. Murdock, "The processing of anthropological materials," 265.
6. George Gaylord Simpson, *The meaning of evolution,* 22–24. See also by the same author: *The geography of evolution;* "The historical factor in science," in *This view of life; Tempo and mode in evolution.*

establishment of Christianity by Constantine and the rise of Islam as revolutions, he was generalizing about two unique events. Modern historians do the same when they write of the English, French, Russian, and Chinese revolutions." In other words, says Carr, "the historian is not really interested in the unique, but what is general in the unique."[7]

Carr is joined by Crane Brinton. To the latter the doctrine of the absolute uniqueness of events in history "seems nonsense." History is essentially "an account of the behavior of men, and if the behavior of men is not subject to any kind of systematizing, this world is even more cock-eyed than the seers would have it." His statement appears in a volume entitled *Anatomy of Revolution* in which the dated episodes of this social phenomenon are regarded as similar enough to be considered as a class of recurrent events.[8]

According to a recent historian of science, Professor Thomas S. Kuhn, the same is no less true with respect to revolutions in scientific thought. Examples with dates, he asserts, may be cited *ad nauseam*, and "they are not isolated events but extended episodes with a regularly recurrent structure."[9] He is joined in this by an earlier historian of science, the late Edgar Zilsel. The lack

of perfect analogies neither speaks against the possibility of historical laws nor does it form a basic difference between history and the natural sciences. . . . True, no two historical individuals are completely alike. . . . However, the repetitions in natural science are overestimated by those only who are rather remote from this field of research. . . . Variety of historico-sociological phenomena surpass variety of other objects in degree only. . . . The conformities in the cultural ideals of Renaissance humanists and Chinese literati-officials can be established first; the differences may be taken into account later.[10]

Among philosophers, similar opinions attesting the presence of classes of like events may be found. Professor Charles Frankel asserts that "if events are the same in some respects, then they are the same in those respects, and that just happens to be that." According to Maurice Mandelbaum, "no historical event could even be described, much less could it be in any sense explained, if it were wholly unique."[11]

7. Edward Hallett Carr, *What is history?* 57. See also Frederick John Teggart, *Theory and processes of history*, 58–64; Charles V. Langlois and Charles Seignobos, *Introduction to the study of history*, 236. "If historical events were literally unique, . . . no [historical] generalizations would be possible . . . and any attempt to understand the past would be entirely futile" (*The social sciences in historical study*, 25); Kenneth Elliot Bock, *The acceptance of histories*, 118–22; William Dray, *Laws and explanation in history*, 44–50.

8. Crane Brinton, *Anatomy of revolution*, 29.

9. Thomas S. Kuhn, *The structure of scientific revolutions*, 52, 135.

10. Edgar Zilsel, "Physics and the problems of historico-sociological laws," 576–77.

11. Maurice Mandelbaum, "Historical explanation: the problem of covering laws," 231; Dray, *Laws and explanation*, 44–50.

Another recent philosopher, Patrick Gardiner, in his discussion of *The Nature of Historical Explanation* reminds his readers that although it is often inferred "that the uniqueness of events . . . excludes the possibility of their being classified or generalized about in any way . . . (or) that they possess some absolute uniqueness which necessitates their being known and explained in a special way," nevertheless, when an historian says

that an event is unique, his statement is incomplete until he states in what respects it is unique. Obviously, the Norman Conquest was unique in the sense that it occurred at a particular time and place, but it was not unique in the sense that events like it, the invasion of one country by another, . . . have occurred on several occasions throughout history.[12]

It was doubtless with such considerations in mind that Professor Edward Strong asserted that the idea of the uniqueness of events is "one whale of an assumption."[13]

Among social anthropologists, Professor Evans-Pritchard has been equally forthright: "No events are unique. The battle of Hastings was only fought once, but it belongs to the 'class' of battles; and it is only when it is so considered that it is intelligible." Events "lose much, even all of their meaning, if they are not seen as having some degree of regularity and constancy, as belonging to a certain type of event, all instances of which have many features in common."[14] The issue of the uniqueness versus the likeness of dated events need no longer halt experimentation by anthropologists with dated materials.

The first and second obstacles to the employment by anthropologists of dated cultural events in the study of social change having thus been considered, it is necessary now to consider a third. This resides in the fact of inexperience, the fact that few anthropologists have attempted to use dated events in this fashion.[15] Consequently, there

---

12. Patrick Gardiner, *The nature of historical explanation*, 41-43. See also Henry Montague Hozier, *The invasions of England*, in which he considers a category of some twenty or more such dated intrusions, or threatened intrusions, into one country; and Frederick John Teggart, *Rome and China*, x, 237, in which the author considers a collection of forty uprisings of the barbarians on the borders of the Roman empire.
13. Edward W. Strong, "How is practice of history tied to theory?" 639.
14. Edward Evan Evans-Pritchard, *Anthropology and history*, 48-49.
15. Alfred Louis Kroeber comes closer than many in his *Configurations of culture growth*. Here he seeks to compare the history, or rather the temporal course, of culture changes as they have terminated from time to time on some areas with the datable phenomenon of civilization. But despite his recognition of the non-narrational character of the procedure which he had adopted, he was unaware of its methodological significance. Consequently, he viewed the uses of "history," first, through the eyes of those diffusionists who "since about 1890," have avowed that the cultural phenomena with which they deal "are properly intelligible only in an historical context" (devoid of dates); or, second, in the spirit of those historians who pause in the construction of selected dated series to describe the culture of certain areas during periods of

has been no adequate taxonomic treatment of dated cultural changes providing the student with appropriate classes of events for study and comparison. There are no well-established guidelines for the choice of the ethnological questions to be put to such classes of events. There is no code of instruction as to how to go to work. There is no insight among anthropologists, as a group of scholarly investigators, into what the results will look like when once they are obtained.

It is a fact, however, that two scholars at least, neither of them anthropologists, have, as the result of their own inspired enterprise, contributed leadership. One of these was the late Professor Frederick J. Teggart, an historian, with his instructive study of the classification and correlation of dated events.[16] The other is Professor Thomas H. Kuhn, a scientist and an historian of science, who having, with others, observed the recurrent character of scientific revolutions, has recently elected to deal with a selected number of dated changes in scientific ideas.[17]

Professor Teggart found his problem in a class of recurrent events well-known to historians as the barbarian invasions of the Roman Empire from 58 B.C. to A.D. 107.[18] However the procedure he adopted to account for this class of datable, historical instances of a similar and repeated human activity was not an educated guess, nor did his treatment of these similar dated events involve the usual composition of a narrative, based upon a selection among them, followed by an inquiry into "causes." To Teggart, the problem seemed rather to call for a complete collection of datable barbarian movements for the period stated followed by another collection of what hypothetically were thought to be prior connecting events: in this case, every war or social disturbance across the Eurasian landmass during the period under review. With the arrangement of both collections in dated order,

---

high civilization (Kroeber's well-known "descriptive interpretations or integrations" or "optional halts for 'topical' discussion"). Though he tried by comparison "to see how the several civilizations . . . behaved alike or unlike in the course of producing their highest manifestations," and though he thus arrived at comparable temporal sequences of activities in these areas, he envisaged these similar temporal sequences in terms of a metaphor, the biological analogy, or as "growths." This ancient conception of cultural change has never been adequately examined by students of the history of ideas, or for its appropriateness as a scientific paradigm, a methodological assumption (4, 6, 663–846). See on the concept of growth, Teggart, *Theory and processes,* 49, 83, 86–87, 91, 95, 98, 100–101, 105, 107, 111, 214–215; "The humanistic study of change in time,"; and "Spengler."

16. Teggart, *Rome and China;* Margaret T. Hodgen, "Frederick John Teggart," xv; 598–99. See also Margaret T. Hodgen, "Geographical diffusion as a criterion of age"; "Glass and paper"; "Similarities and dated distributions"; *Change and history;* "Anthropology, history and science."

17. Thomas S. Kuhn, *The structure of scientific revolutions.*

18. Teggart, *Rome and China,* vii.

followed by their comparison as categories of events, the result seemed
to be unmistakable and definite. Common features were elicited
suggesting significant relationships. Within the chosen decades, according to Teggart, "every barbarian uprising in Europe followed
the outbreak of war either on the eastern frontiers of the Roman
Empire or in the 'Western Regions' of the Chinese."[19] Thus, the
primary result of this twofold classification of two supposedly unique
events was the establishment of *correlations* in classes of dated events.
Though, in referring to these results, Professor Teggart himself
preferred the term "process" to that of "law," the eminent historian
of science, the late Edgar Zilsel, declared that the correlation among
dated events disclosed in the book, *Rome and China,* "constituted
the first statement of an historical law achieved with the necessary
scientific accuracy."[20]

Professor Teggart's work on historical phenomena in Eurasia during
a period in antiquity is obviously several removes from the current
interests of most students of primitive cultures. Nevertheless, since
both he and they are deeply concerned with the same question, namely
a valid and scientific approach to the phenomena of social change,
his refutation of the dogma of the uniqueness of the dated events
of change, together with his discovery of regularities and correlations
in classes of events, serves not only as an encouragement but as
a milestone in both historical and anthropological thought. In Teggart's
view, like results are attainable again and again if only other historical
and cultural questions are similarly approached with some semblance
"to the patient care exercised in the study of an atom of hydrogen."[21]

Professor Kuhn's interests are also nonanthropological, unless the
history of scientific ideas, or of changes in scientific thought, be
considered an anthropological problem and a necessary part therefore
of the study of advanced cultures. The reader will find that Kuhn
is concerned with determining the *historical* structure of changes in
scientific ideas, or with the detection of the *regularly* manifested
sequence of recorded events and conditions which bring new ideas
into being. Such an interest throws him immediately into the history
of basic scientific concepts, principles of organization, assumptions,
traditional patterns of inquiry, or what he prefers to call paradigms.[22]

19. Ibid., vii, 236.
20. Zilsel, "Physics and historico-sociological laws," 575 n.5.
21. Teggart, *Rome and China,* vii; see also Teggart, "Anthropology and history"
and "The humanistic study of change in time."
22. "These I take to be universally recognized scientific achievements that for a
time provide model problems and solutions to a community of practitioners" (Kuhn,
Structure of scientific revolutions, x.)

By comparing certain selected[23] historical and dated episodes of change from one paradigm to another, and by attempting thus to elicit similar elements in the process, he reaches the conclusion that all scientific revolutions are the outcome of a common sequence of events. Stated in a summary fashion, this sequence begins (1) with an awareness on the part of one or more scientists of an anomaly in an old paradigm;[24] followed by (2) its adjustment, or a transition into a new paradigm; initiated by (3) individual scientists;[25] who (4) slowly obtain the acceptance of a new paradigm among the members of the scientific community by a process not unlike conversion.[26]

Thus Kuhn's objective is to attain from a study of the dated and recorded past of scientific thought a concept of the history of science, or of change in scientific thought, different from the stereotypes repetitiously stated in science texts, or in traditional narrative and linear science history.[27] To him, these old fashioned stereotypes are based largely upon a concept of change by accumulation, and have had a tendency "to force nature into conceptual boxes supplied by professional education."[28] Thus, as a result, normal, customary, conventional or day-to-day scientific inquiry "does not aim at novelties of fact or theory and, when successful, finds none." Normal or conventional research "owes its success to the ability of scientists regularly to select problems that can be solved with conceptual and instrumental techniques close to those already in existence."[29] Revolutionary changes in scientific ideas, on the other hand, are taken to be those noncumulative episodes "in which an older paradigm is replaced in whole or part by an incompatible new one,"[30] just as a political revolution compels the relinquishment of one set or system of social institutions for another.

What, then, is the bearing of the work of these two men, Teggart and Kuhn, upon the work of the anthropologist, or perhaps upon some wayward historian? Suppose, with them, he abandons the conventional assumption that dated human history, as studied and

23. Since his most fundamental objective was to urge a change in the perception and evaluation of familiar data, he regarded the essentially schematic character of his first presentation of the plan as no drawback. "Far more historical evidence is available than I have had space to exploit . . ." (Ibid., xi). "I have so far tried to explain revolutions by *illustration* (Italics added), and the examples could be multiplied *ad nauseam*" (Ibid., 135).
24. Ibid., 52.
25. Ibid., 143.
26. Ibid., 150.
27. Ibid., 1.
28. Ibid., 5.
29. Ibid., 52, 95.
30. Ibid., 91.

written, is logically continuous with literature (or narrative) rather than with science? Suppose he takes the position that history, defined as the total dated and documented record of the human past, is a far broader subject than that envisioned by narrative and literary historians? Suppose the corpus of dated documentation be thought of, not as the private and inviolable treasury of those who desire to accomplish some literary design, but rather as a mammoth file, open to all, of still unarranged dated records of possibly repeated experiments by men to alter or change their condition? Suppose, in contrast to the documentary riches of the historian, the anthropologist recognizes the documentary poverty of the naturalist's approach to a parallel problem, and decides to forego dealing with the process of change as naturalists are forced to do? Suppose he listens to those who assure him of the presence in the historical record of the recurrence of many dated cultural changes, extending over centuries, and related to many large or small geographical and cultural regions? Suppose, convinced of the likeness and classifiability of at least *some* dated events of cultural change, and emancipated from ancient paradigms such as the several conventional philosophies of history, he favors the acceptance of a concept of scientific method which calls, first, for the collection of dated changes; moves on from there to their classification; and then, when possible, attempts to find their correlation with other promising classes of prior dated events? How may he set about handling these, to him, new materials in a new way? What kinds of results may he anticipate?

It is at this point that the study of cultural change, so central to the social studies and to many of the humanities, may be modestly and effectively reopened, unconstrained by conventional and paradigmatic value judgments as to their future direction; or by a priori philosophies of history, including envisagements of cultural change as variations on the theme of organic "growth," as developmental or evolutionary.

CHAPTER 4

The Classification of Dated Cultural Events:
An Alternative Use of History Illustrated

The initial steps to be taken by anthropologists or historians in this venture are, first, the acquirement of an appropriate and *inclusive* collection of more than one category of dated cultural changes or innovations, secondly, the separation within each category of differences or similarities, and, thirdly, in the presence of similarities of event-marked innovations in hand, the search for common antecedents or conditions.

In acquiring inclusive collections of dated cultural changes, the novice is given two options: (1) he may decide to start de novo, as himself the collector,[1] a time-consuming procedure but one sooner or later to be faced as inevitable; or (2) he may accept collections of dated events of similar cultural changes already assembled.

Happily, for making a start, or for adding a few more pilot studies to those already published,[2] there have long been groups of scholars (some, indeed, may have been called historians) who have abstained from narration in favor of the collection of similar historical artifacts,

---

1. This was the choice adopted by Frederick John Teggart in dealing with the recurrent events of the barbarian invasions. ". . . It at once became necessary to assemble all the data which might be supposed to have a bearing upon the occurrences in question" (of which there were 40 consecutive instances in a period of 165 years from 58 B.C. to A.D. 107). With this object in view, the procedure adopted was first "to set down in chronological order all known events, wars, and disturbances, *in each separate kingdom* or region of the continent of Eurasia. . . . The compilation of data for every country from Britain to Cambodia took the form of separate chronological lists, and the next, though long delayed, step in the investigation was to set these lists side by side and compare the occurrences in geographical order across the map of Eurasia" (*Rome and China*, vii, 244).

2. Teggart, *Rome and China*. Also Margaret T. Hodgen, "Geographical diffusion as a criterion of age"; "Glass and paper"; "Similarities and dated distributions"; *Change and history*.

documents, or events to assist in narration. In bibliographies, such titles often appear under the rubric of handbooks, manuals, gazetteers, atlases, and the like,[3] some of which have no other object than to draw up minute inventories of like events, or like acquisitions made to knowledge. Among such historical collectors there are numismatists, for example, who collect coins both for the sake of collection and to aid in dating historical events. There are archaeologists whose collections and gazetteers of excavated artifacts come to the assistance of the historian seeking to recover periods for which written records are scarce or absent. There are collections of dated place-names which may lend certainty to the localization of some types of recorded events, or contribute to the cultural description of historical periods.

There are handbooks of universal history, such as Putnam's,[4] containing personally selected "major" events in various geographical areas, chronologically arranged and presented, for ease in comparison, in parallel columns. There are histories of architecture, art, painting, and sculpture so detailed as to facilitate the collection of all, or nearly all, of the events associated with the introduction of new forms or techniques in the Greek, Roman, Carolingian, Norman, Baroque, Oriental, and other styles in many areas. There are dictionaries of battles which make the study of this class of events feasible from some points of view. There are publications, such as the *Victoria History of the Counties of England,* replete with information necessary to date and place innovations of various kinds: water mills, fairs, religious houses, trades and handicrafts, to mention only a few.

There are literatures of social institutions such as the Parliamentary form of government and other forms; of the learned and antiquarian societies; of the monasteries and universities; many of which are so exhaustively accompanied with facts concerning dates and places of first establishment as to make them appropriate and tempting fields for the study of historical (rather than preliterate) cultural changes.

Among many of the compilers of such literatures, though their collections may yield the dates of events, collection is an end in itself. Their purposes are fulfilled without making these dated categories the subject of cultural inquiry. For others their collections are ready for newer types of classificatory investigation.

At all events, though none of these possibilities may appeal to

3. Vivian H. Galbraith, *An introduction to the study of history,* 22-47; Charles V. Langlois and Charles Seignobos, *Introduction to the study of history,* 17-55, 101-107, 307-310.
4. George Palmer Putnam, *Putnam's handbook of universal history.*

every anthropo-historian, their existence and plurality demonstrate
that the collection of similar dated cultural events is not a dangerously
radical undertaking.[5] The major missing ingredient is a plan for using
them (or others) in statements of an anthropological problem requiring
an historico-scientific solution, or of correlating classes of dated
changes with classes of antecedent dated events or conditions.

In order to indicate some of the more obvious elements involved
in the anthropological study of classes of dated changes in culture,
I have decided to forego the protracted procedure of compiling classes
of dated changes de novo. Instead, use will be made of two collections
already in being. One of these is in the field of printing technology.
Compiled by bibliographers of the earliest printed books, or incunabula,[6] it deals also with the presses which produced them, giving the
dates and places at which they were first established, for a period
of five decades in the fifteenth century, or from 1450 to 1500.[7] The
second is the ready-to-hand collection in the field of the history of
the institution of religion. Here, eminent students of the ancient history
of the Christian faith have elected to establish the places and dates
of the formation of every Christian group, or "church," from the
year A.D. 1 to the year 400, or for four hundred years.[8]

Each of these collections is intended to be as exhaustive with
reference to dates, places, individuals concerned, and other features
as highly trained, specialized historical scholarship can make them.[9]
The most recent body of dated material dealing with an example
of religious change in culture comes not from a narrative history
but from a noteworthy publication on the order of a gazetteer or
atlas. In van der Meer and Mohrmann's *Atlas of the Early Christian
World* (1858) the anthropological student of religious change is given

5. Margaret T. Hodgen, *Early anthropology in the sixteenth and seventeenth centuries,*
Chapter V on the "Collection of customs," 162-206. See also Peter R. Gould, *Spatial
diffusion,* 1-71.
6. A book printed before 1501.
7. Chief sources for collection: Henry Cotton, *A typographical gazetteer;* Henry
Cotton, *A typographical gazetteer . . .* 2d Series; *Catalogue of books printed in the
XVth century now in the British Museum;* Konrad Haebler, *The early printers of Spain
and Portugal.* See also Anatole Claudin, *Les origines de l'imprimerie en France;* Polydore
Charles van der Meersch, *Recherches sur la vie et les travauxes imprimeurs belges
et neerlandais;* Mario Emilio Cosenza, *Biographical and bibliographical dictionary of
the Italian printers;* Konrad Haebler, *The study of incunabula;* Bernard Alexander
Uhlendorf, "The invention of printing and its spread until 1470"; Elizabeth L. Eisenstein,
"The advent of printing and the problem of the Renaissance."
8. Chief sources for the collection: Carl Gustav Adolf von Harnack, *The mission
and expansion of Christianity in the first three centuries;* Frederick van der Meer and
Christine Mohrmann, *Atlas of the early Christian world.*
9. Criticism of the obvious incompatibilities of these two collections of dated events
should not be too harsh until the critic has tried to make a collection de novo for
himself.

a geographical and dated index of all the known churches or Christian groups in the Mediterranean and European world, beginning with post-apostolic times in the first century A.D. and extending to A.D. 600, a period of time during which the Greek east lost "its hinterlands" and the Latin west saw "the disappearance of classical society."[10] The earliest "churches" (often in private houses) known to have existed in the first century included those "founded by Peter and Paul and those mentioned in Revelations 1-2. . . . The earliest documents are those of the New Testament and the letter of Clement."[11] Included also are "all Christian bishoprics except those lying far outside the imperial boundaries, notably in the Parthian kingdom and farther east."[12]

When the details of these two categories of dated cultural changes, the presses and the Christian groups, have been transferred to cards for ease in sub-classification; or, putting it in another way, when these two *species* (in the biological sense), or classes of *dated events* (in the historical sense), or *dated classes of cultural changes* (in the anthropological sense) have been sorted according to various criteria; when, so sorted, they have been organized in tabular form or plotted on maps, some similarities, common features, or regularities do emerge.

For example, no one knows how many cities, towns, villages, hamlets, or other organized human groupings existed in Renaissance Europe, or in the world around the eastern Mediterranean at the beginning of the Christian era. Nevertheless, it is plain that these two datable cultural changes, the printing press and the Christian congregation, were not geographically universal. Over the two periods of historical time under review, the printing press with movable metal type did not appear, or "evolve," in every European community; nor did the followers of Jesus announce discipleship in every town and village around the Mediterranean. Principles of selection were at work. When changes occurred, according to the dated record, only a fraction of all the known organized communities became the sites of one or the other of these innovations.[13] For some reason or reasons

10. van der Meer and Mohrmann, *Atlas of the Christian world*, 5.
11. Ibid., 213.
12. Ibid., 8.
13. To statisticians many of the dated numerical facts elicited in this study may seem too small to be of significance. They are urged to reconsider the work of the *science* of paleontology from the same point of view. According to George Gaylord Simpson, for example, "information on the earlier mammals is still extremely scanty. Only about a *dozen* forms (Italics added), scattered from the late Eocene or Oligocene through the Pliocene have as yet been described. . . . In conservative classification there are six living and two recently extinct families of Australian marsupials, etc. . . ." (*The geography of evolution*, 154-55). It is upon such evidence that many findings

the people of only a few communities, during these two periods, welcomed the new traits. The majority did not. Thus the first and most obvious sorting of these two classes of events is numerical and geographical, in response to the questions: How many communities adopted the printing press or Christian belief for the *first*[14] time during the period under consideration? Where were they? How were these first acceptances, or cultural changes, distributed temporally and spatially?[15] The contemporary, twentieth-century cultural scene in the western world and in the undeveloped nations is commonly supposed to be one of rapid and ever more rapid change. But how fast did cultural changes take place in the past, and how do rates differ for different regions, for different items of culture, at different historical periods? There is little or nothing known on such subjects because, in the first place, most anthropological studies of cultural change are focused on contemporary primitive societies and their more or less recent responses to western ideas and artifacts; and, in the second place, all such studies cover very restricted spans of

---

in historical geology have been reached. Those fractions of all human settlements which accepted the innovations of the printing press and the new religion may also be helpfully compared, for illustrative purposes, to the fractions of biological species which undergo viable mutation, and from which biologists draw at least some of their conclusions. It should also be pointed out again that these two collections of the events of cultural changes now under consideration, *are not samples*, statistically devised. Like the scanty fossil remains, mentioned above, they each include *all* recorded cases known to the best informed scholars.

14. The *first* appearance of a trait in a community culture is emphasized, despite possible subsequent appearances in the same community, because in the latter case they are repetitions of the innovation and the innovating impulse. (See Hodgen, "Primary and secondary innovators," in *Change and history*, 92-96.) A little reflection on the part of the reader will convince him that although other acceptances of the same new trait may well follow its first acceptance in a community, and the new trait may thereby be multiplied on a given site, the number of new sites, or new changing communities, will not be multiplied. In Venice, for example, where the first press appeared in 1469, "some 150 presses opened their doors in thirty-one years, an average of nearly five firms a year from 1469 to 1501" (Curt Ferdinand Bühler, *The fifteenth century book*, 54-55). Yet the installation of the first one was the change of greatest significance in the community. All others merely indicate continuing approval of the new technology and are therefore ignored in the discussion to follow. (For further comment on this point see Hodgen, "Similarities and dated distributions," 450-53.) It should be noted that when a similar problem of procedure arises in historical geology or paleontology, a similar solution is reached. The data available to the paleontologist, says Professor Simpson, "are (historical) records of the occurrence of the various taxonomic entities within each period. . . . Strictly speaking the factual data do not include times of origin or of extinction, but only the times of *first* and *last* appearance in the record as known. . . . *First appearances . . . are accepted as more nearly objective and basic* (Italics added) than opinions as to the time when each group really originated" (Simpson, *Geography of evolution*, 18-19).

15. The statistical term *distribution* is preferred to the anthropological term *diffusion*. The former is taken to express a temporal or geographical fact attested by dated evidence and/or maps; the latter is a general explanation or a theory of how these distributed facts happened to occur as they did in time or space.

Table 1. Numbers and Rates of Increase or Decrease in the First
Community Acceptances of the Printing Press

Printing Presses

Dated Period (A.D.)	Number of New Accepting Communities by Decade	Per Cent of Total for the Period
1450–59	1	—
1460–69	11	4
1470–79	97	39
1480–89	89	36
1490–99	50	20
	248	100

recent time.[16] That being the case, there is no reason (unless the student resorts to the very shaky assumption of uniformitarianism) to think that what has happened recently, or during the last three, ten, fifty, or one hundred years in some preliterate culture is true also for what has happened in any advanced culture during the last five hundred, one thousand, or five thousand years.[17]

Dealing then with the actual numbers and rates of increase or decrease in new printing communities or Christian communities for the periods under review, it may be that during the last half of the fifteenth century, or from 1450 to 1500, when printing by movable metal type was first introduced into western Europe, the number of accepting, or changing communities, reached a grand total of 248 (Table 1 and Map A 1). Within that fifty-year period the number and rate of new community acceptances, decade by decade, both increased and decreased. That is to say, during the first two decades (or more properly, during the first 12 years) it increased from 1 in Mainz in 1457[18] to 11 at other sites by the end of 1469 (Map A2). These 11 added communities were Strasbourg in 1460, Bamberg in 1461, Foligno

16. See the discussion of procedures by more or less contemporary students of cultural change on pp. 17–21.

17. George Gaylord Simpson has much the same to say concerning rates of change among biological organisms. "There is no such thing as *the* rate of evolution. . . . The record has demonstrated that evolution is not some over-all cosmic influence that has been changing all living things in a regular way throughout the periods of the earth's history. Some groups have been changed rapidly while others were remaining practically unchanged. The same group is commonly seen to have changed rapidly at some times in its history and slowly or not at all in others (*The meaning of evolution,* 97 ff. For a discussion dealing with rates of change in prehistoric biological forms, see George Gaylord Simpson, *Tempo and mode in evolution,* 3 ff).

18. On the controversy as to whether Haarlem was the site of the first press, see *Catalogue of books printed in the XVth century,* IX: xxi–xxvi.

⊙ Mainz

Map A 1. Total distribution of the sites of newly established printing presses, A.D. 1457 to 1499, with a few important thirteenth century roadways.

presses *
Mainz press ⊛
major roads ····

Map A 2. Distribution of new sites of printing presses, for the earliest period from 1457 to 1469.

49

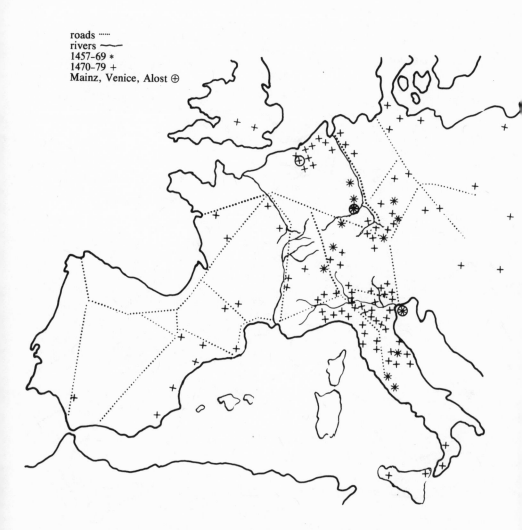

roads ·····
rivers ⌒
1457–69 *
1470–79 +
Mainz, Venice, Alost ⊕

Map A 3. New sites of printing presses for the two earliest decades, 1457–69 and 1470–79.

Map A 4. New sites of printing presses for the decade 1480 to 1489.

Map A 5. New sites of printing presses for the decade 1490 to 1499.

in 1463, Subiaco in Italy in 1465, Cologne in 1466, Rome and Eltville in 1467, Basel and Augsburg in 1468, Venice in 1469, and Nürnberg before 1470. But during the next decade, or from 1470 to 1479, the popularity of movable type increased rapidly. It found its way into 97 additional communities, or from 4 per cent to 39 per cent of the grand total for the five-decade period. At this juncture, however, a decline set in of about 3 per cent which, in the next decade, was continued. From 1490 to 1499 only 50 new communities were made the sites of the new press, a figure which was only 20 per cent of the total accepted during the entire half century under review.

Similar observations may be made with reference to the collection of dated events referring to new community acceptances of Christian doctrine, or the geographical sites of new Christian congregations,[19] a cultural change even more sharply divergent from the customary mores of many areas than the introduction of movable type.

At the end of the four-century period under examination (or from A.D. 1 to A.D. 399), and after persistent missionization, the total number of communities newly practicing the rites of Christianity around the Mediterranean (out of the thousands of human settlements seemingly appropriate for the appearance of the phenomenon of religious conversion) was nevertheless only 698 (Table 2; Map B1). The rate of acceptance over this period of time, however, was an increasing one with no declines in any century.[20] As for differences in the comparative rates of the community acceptance of presses and congregations on *new* sites, congregations increased faster than presses and, in the end, may have far surpassed the number of new communities which adopted presses.

19. The classification of Christianized communities by decade, or by the use of a temporal unit less than 100 years, is not practical. Many dated events marking this religious change are derived from single documents, such as lists of bishops present at the Synod of Carthage in A.D. 256 or at the Council of Nicaea in A.D. 325, and stating the localities they represented. For this reason, the figures cited for the distribution of the printing presses (classified by decade), and those of Christian congregations (classified by century), are probably incomparable, especially since the former study covers only five decades, while the latter covers four hundred years. However, the spans of five decades in the one case and four centuries in the other are both, broadly speaking, introductory periods in eventual worldwide distributions, and deserve attention on that account alone. Moreover, as *introductory* periods, they show similar phenomena. Nor is it thinkable that a historical geologist, given both a short and a long chronology of fossil forms, would refrain from comparing them just because the span of documentation differed in length.

20. For still other rates of acceptance of new traits, see Hodgen, "Similarities and dated distributions," 452–53.

Table 2. Numbers and Rates of First Community Acceptances of Christian
Doctrine

Dated Period A.D.	Number of New Accepting Communities	Per Cent of Total for the Period
1–99	61	8
100–199	77	11
200–299	136	19
300–399	424	60

Beginning with the formation of the first group of disciples in Jerusalem immediately after the Crucifixion in the year A.D. 33, and throughout the remainder of the first century, it would seem that the new faith, as understood by apostles, missionaries, and other zealots, had already been made available to the whole Mediterranean world.[21] The dated facts, however, indicate something less in terms of actual or recorded community acceptances. At the end of the first century, or after approximately 67 years of evangelistic effort, congregations had appeared in only 61, or 8 per cent of the four-century total, of Christian communities (Map B1). The sites of these first Christianized groups are to be observed as geographically distributed in the towns of Galilee and Samaria; on the sea coast of Judea; in Asia Minor, Greece, and Italy (Rome, Puteoli, and possibly Pompeii);[22] in North Africa (Cyrene and Alexandria); and in the upper Tigris and Euphrates region (Edessa, or Urfa, and Beit Zabde)[23] (Map B2).

By the end of the second century of distribution, or from A.D. 100 to A.D. 199, 77 additional communities were added, or 11 per cent of the four-century total of new sites. In the third century this figure was almost doubled to 136, or 19 per cent, while in the fourth and final century the number of new communities offering hospitality

21. According to the Book of Acts 2:9–11, written in A.D. 64, there were "Parthians and Medes and Elamites, and the dwellers in Mesopotamia, and in Judea, and Cappadocia, in Pontus, and Asia, Phyrgia, and Pamphylia, in Egypt and parts of Libya about Cyrene, and strangers from Rome, Jews, Proselytes, Cretes, and Arabians" telling the works of God (*The interpreter's Bible* . . ., IX:40–41).

22. Kenneth Scott Latourette, *A history of the expansion of Christianity*, I:82; van der Meer and Mohrmann, Map 1.

23. van der Meer and Mohrmann, 188, 191. See also Walter F. Adeney, *The Greek and eastern churches*, 295 ff.

Map B 1. The total distribution of newly established sites of Christian congregations for the four-century period A.D. 1–399.

to members of the new faith had leaped to 424, or 60 per cent of the total[24] (Table 2).

Judging, however, by the more detailed records of dates from the fourth century, this general and steady increase in the number of Christianized communities was not continuous, evenly distributed year by year or decade by decade. Like the dated record of the introduction of the printing presses, the breakdown of dates during the first four centuries of Christianization, shows numerical discontinuities, irregularities, or gaps. In one decade, for example, from A.D. 330 to 339, there is a record of as few as two new communities in which Christian congregations were organized; while in another decade, that from 320 to 329, there were as many as 120.[25]

Turning now from the numerical to the spatial aspects of these two classes of dated events of cultural changes, the presses and the congregations, it will be helpful to consider the geographical distribution of each class, first, in general, or over the whole period of collection (Maps A1 and B1); and second, during the several subperiods already employed (Maps A2-4 and B2-5). This done, it will be found that (1) with the passage of time, or during the sequences of subperiods, the geographical distribution of both innovations took a westerly rather than easterly direction;[26] that (2) each distribution started from an originally small region or cluster; that (3) occasional and apparently random acceptances occurred at unusual distances from the original cluster; and that (4) these instances of acceptance "at a distance"[27] became, as time went on, the geographical *foci* for the formation of *additional* geographical clusters of changing communities.

Since the number of communities which failed to accept either the printing press or the new religion was much larger than the number which did, it becomes a matter of some concern to elicit the facts and patterns of this "selection" geographically. Where, in other words, were these two new culture traits welcomed, and where were they rejected, or not offered for acceptance? The geographical patterns of the distribution of the culturally new around the Mediterranean, or in western Europe, may be equally or even more rewarding than

24. For a discussion of the difficulties of obtaining this kind of information, see Latourette, *A history of Christianity*, I:66 ff.

25. Compare the presence of these temporal discontinuities in the rate of cultural changes with the discontinuities in organic forms as discussed by Simpson, *Tempo and mode in evolution*, 97-148.

26. For exceptions to this statement see Map B1 and the presence of Christian congregations in the Tigris and Euphrates valley, east of Judea.

27. A similar phenomenon has been observed in preceding studies. For discussion of other distributions "at a distance," see Hodgen, "Similarities and dated distributions," 460-63.

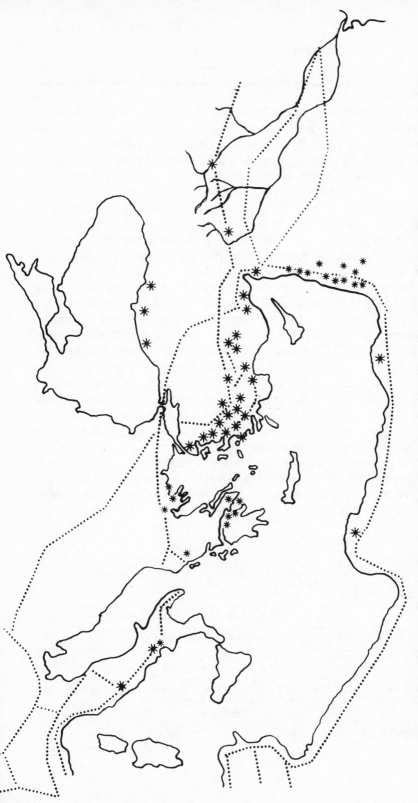

Map B 2. Distribution of new sites of Christian congregations during the first century, or about A.D. 33 to 99, with some of the main Roman roads.

the numerical distributions just discussed, and therefore merit sustained attention.

Turning then to the Maps A1 and B1 showing the *total* geographical distributions of each of the two innovations for the *total* periods under consideration, there is at first relatively little to say. Though the ultimate distribution of the printing press in the twentieth century has proved to be world-wide, it appeared at the end of its fifth decade in the fifteenth century to be confined to a rather narrow band across Europe from Italy to the English Channel, or in a central continental[28] region, bounded roughly in the west by the Rhone and Seine rivers and in the east by the Elbe. This distribution thins out toward the west in France and Spain; and in the east between the Rhine and the Elbe.

The map of the total distribution of Christian congregations at the end of the fourth century (Map B1), like that of the total distribution of presses, is also somewhat inexpressive. Nevertheless, from the territorial standpoint it does record not only many of the conversion sites of Paul's first journey, with many of those which followed,[29] but also the distribution of continuing successful evangelical effort by an increasing number of Christian converts. By 399 the Christian religion had been accepted not only across the heartland of Europe but also in at least four other easily distinguishable clusters: one in southern Spain, one in Tunisian North Africa, another in Asia Minor and along the Judean coast of the Mediterranean, with important extensions westward into Greece and south and east into the Nile Valley and the Valley of the Tigris and Euphrates rivers (Map B1).

Paul's first journey began in A.D. 43 or 45, about ten years after Calvary. As the result of his efforts, and those of later apostles and

---

28. The printing press was not taken across the Channel to England until the eighth decade of the fifteenth century: to Westminster in 1474, to Oxford in 1478, and to St. Albans in 1479. Meanwhile, by the end of the same decade 97 continental communities had accepted the press (Table 1).

29. The dates of Paul's missionary journeys: first, ca. 43–47 A.D.; second, ca. 48–52; third, ca. 54–59; arrest and imprisonment, 59–61; voyage to Rome 61–64. These journeys covered a period of 16 years from ca. 43–64 A.D. (Joseph Klausner: *From Jesus to Paul*, 351,371,385.) For other possible dates of these events, see Benjamin Vincent Haydyn *Dictionary of dates and universal information relating to all ages and nations;* Harnack, *Mission and expansion*, I:45 and notes 1, 2; Latourette, *A history of Christianity*, 69. Paul's efforts were, of course, preceded by those of the group of The Twelve, to which Luke adds another seventy. The Twelve were composed of Simon bar Jonah (later called Cephas or Peter), Andrew, James and John (sons of Zebedee), Philip, Bartholomew, Matthew (or Levi), Thomas (or Didymus), James (son of Alphaeus), Jude, Simon (the Canaanite, also called "the Zealot"), and Judas Iscariot (replaced by Matthias). After the crucifixion, James, a brother of Jesus was reckoned as an apostle (*Standard Jewish Encyclopedia*,35-36).

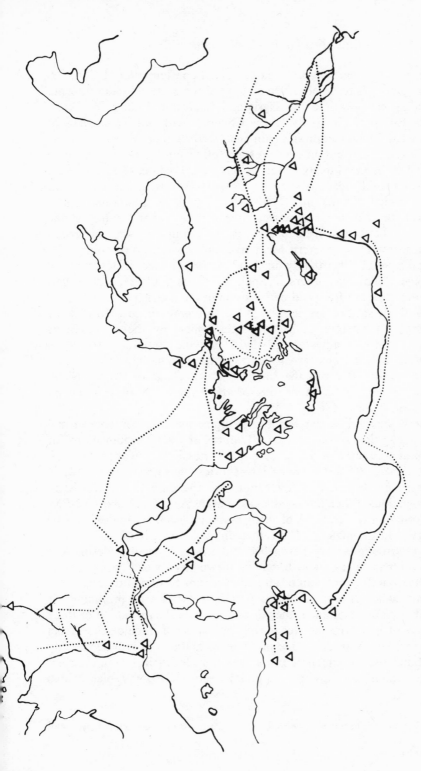

Map B 3. Distribution of new sites of Christian congregations during the second century, or A.D. 100 to 199, with some of the main Roman roads.

missionaries of many types, a large spatial configuration of Christian congregations is to be observed all around the eastern Mediterranean, extending sparsely into the Tigris and Euphrates Valley, in a band across Europe from Sicily to the Channel, with important signs of successful dissemination in Spain and North Africa (Map B1).

This total distribution also presents other configurations of some interest. It includes many lesser regions all around the Mediterranean, north and south, responsive to the Gospel—Palestine, Greece, Egypt, Italy, France, Spain, and North Africa, with an additional scatter in Gaul, or mid-Europe, between the Rhone and the Seine on the west and the Rhine on the east. It is marked also by the clusterings of sites: one in the eastern Mediterranean, composed of community acceptances of Christianity in Asia Minor, Greece, Palestine, and the Nile Delta; two others in Spain and North Africa; and a third crossing northern Italy and mid-Europe to the English Channel.

All of these clusters are bounded by more or less formidable geographical barriers: in eastern Asia Minor, by the mountainous sources of the headwaters of the Tigris and Euphrates rivers; in Palestine, by the trans-Jordan wastes of the Syrian desert; in Greece, by the Danube River to the north; in Carthaginian or Roman North Africa, by the Atlas Mountains or the Sahara; in mid-Europe by the Rhine River to the east.

The discussion so far has turned upon the rates of change and the geographical or distributional features of the two innovations for the *total* period under investigation. It is possible, however, to break down these total distributions into shorter time units, by decade in the case of the presses, by century in the case of the Christian congregations. When this is done (as in Maps A2-A5 and Maps B2-B5), the formation of clusters of change-accepting communities may be observed in the making. The rather unintelligible scatters of the two total distributions may be spelled out into a kind of orderliness.[30] The two map series, indeed, may be viewed as a visual, geographical (and temporal) exposition of an active cluster-forming process.

Thus, when the maps of the first two decades of printing-press distribution are examined, they display at once the formation of three clusters of new printing sites during the course of three decades from 1450 to 1479 (Map A3). One of these formations is around the city of Mainz (where the first press was introduced in 1457). Another cluster seems to follow the River Po westward from Venice (which

30. For similar phenomena, see Hodgen, "Similarities and dated distributions," 461.

Map B 4. The distribution of new sites of Christian congregations during the third century, or from A.D. 200 to 299.

received its first press in 1469), while a third makes its appearance in the Low Countries after the founding of a press at Alost in 1473.[31] Both Venice and Alost were sites of acceptance "at a distance" with reference to the first site, Mainz, and in turn became the first members of new geographical clusters. Subsequent maps show the same clusters growing more concentrated and expanding into one another, until a final more generalized distribution is reached in the last decade of the fifteenth century, or in 1490–99 (Maps A1–A5).

Analysis of the Christian sequence of "century" maps shows the probable presence of the operation of a similar geographical and temporal process. After the earlier efforts of the closer followers of Jesus had been exercised in Judea immediately after the Crucifixion, sparse anticipations of the formation of other Christian groups began to appear. One of these in the second century was on the northern tributaries of the Tigris and Euphrates rivers, and is an instance of cluster formation around a site of "acceptance at a distance," or at Edessa (Urfa) (Maps B2 and B3). Other instances may be observed around Rome, in Roman or Carthaginian North Africa, and in Europe on lands drained by the Rhone and the Rhine. In the third century all of these potential foci of clusters, the earliest in Judea and the later ones elsewhere, showed expansion, except for those in Greece and Asia Minor, where Paul had already converted so many souls. In the fourth century, expansion was accelerated everywhere except in North Africa[32] and in the Tigris-Euphrates region. New congregations were established widely in barbarian Europe, especially in Northern Italy, Southern Spain, and Macedonia, but only sparsely across the Mediterranean in Northern Africa and in the region of the great river system of the ancient civilizations of the Medes and Persians (Map B5).

In summary then, when temporal and geographical distributions of the two classes of dated events marking the acceptance of the new presses and the new Christian doctrine are considered together (having first been divided into dated "periods," and so mapped), several common distributional features may be observed. The region in which each innovation was first introduced, or "tried out," was small. It frequently happened that the event of the first acceptance

31. *Catalogue of books printed in the XVth century,* IX: viii, 125.
32. The documentation for this period in North Africa is scanty, and may account for the apparent decline of new Christian groups as reflected on Map B5. Competent students point out, however, that it was a time when the number of bishoprics probably doubled. "In 312 there were at least 70 in Numidia alone, and by 330, the Donatists could number two hundred and seventy" (B. H. Warmington, *The North African provinces from Diocletian to the Vandal conquest,* 76). See also Frederik van der Meer, *Augustine the bishop.*

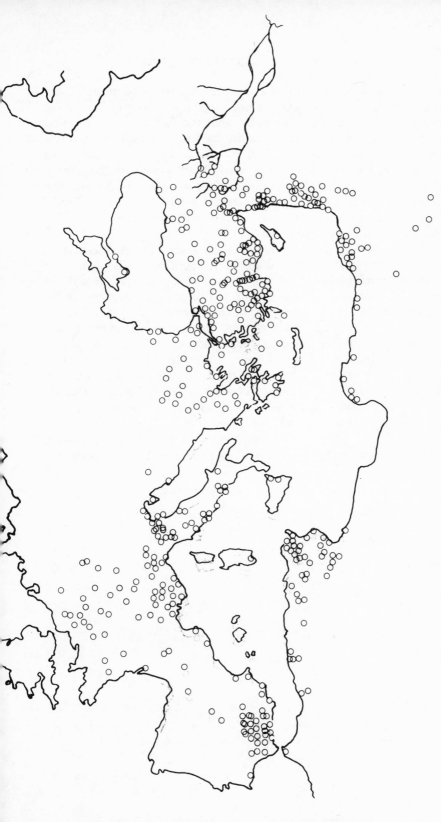

Map B 5. Distribution of new sites of Christian congregations in the fourth century, or A.D. 300 to 399.

occurred at a single, or ''original'' site, and was followed in a relatively short time by new sites forming a nearby group or cluster of accepting communities. It appears, secondly, that the formation of this first geographical cluster was accompanied by a few acceptances in a few communities ''at a distance,'' or too far away to be regarded as members of the first cluster. It appears, thirdly, that with the passage of time and the continued acceptability of the new traits by an expanding number of communities, the communities involved exhibited a well-defined tendency to cluster around these acceptances ''at a distance,''[33] forming additional well-defined clusters.

Thus these early dated cultural changes around the Mediterranean, when temporally classified and considered geographically, negate the widely-entertained belief (according to an old paradigm) that dated events fall more smoothly into some sort of order dictated by merely literary selection, or narrative form. On the contrary, they fall easily into temporal and geographical classes. They not only tend to increase moderately in numbers but characteristically in space, and this simple temporal increase and geographical spread (at least for the brief dated periods under review) *fail completely to uphold the assumption of the universality of specific cultural changes, as implied in many theories of cultural evolution.* At the same time, neither the temporal increases nor the geographical spreads are random or formless; nor do they suggest the relevance of the simplistic theory of radiation from a center of initial change presupposed by the age-and-area hypothesis.

33. Hodgen, ''Similarities and dated distributions,'' 460–61.

CHAPTER 5

Historical Process Versus Natural Law as Forms of Explanation

Cultural changes are not propelled from place to place on wings. They have not occurred every day in past time nor everywhere in geographical space. Yet, as indicated by the foregoing tables and maps, their temporal appearances present determinable profiles, and their locations in inhabited territories fall into describable sequences of spatial configurations.

How are these cultural phenomena, these results of the classification of the dated events of cultural changes, these newly elicited dated classes, temporal and spatial similarities, these empirically determined "regularities" or configurations, to be explained, accounted for, or made more intelligible?

The theory of cultural development or evolution upon which many anthropologists lean so heavily in their discussion of cultural changes is rapidly becoming irrelevant. In the first place, as a so-called natural law paralleling or expressed in a series continuing the organic series of the biologist, it is a statement of what happens naturally or normally in abstraction from what actually happened in the form of supposedly unique events.[1] Secondly, its good repute has been tarnished by its intellectual entanglement in the social studies with the long discredited but still not abandoned Comparative or Historical Method.[2] The

1. "The high abstraction from the particularity and individuality of objects as found in experience which logicians have insisted upon as the dominant characteristic of all scientific work," is not distinctive of the historical studies, human or geological (Frederick John Teggart, *Theory and processes of history*, 165-68); the anthropologists and sociologists "who are seeking for a universal natural history of society or culture subject to natural law simply are not reckoning with the empirical facts of history" (David Bidney, *Theoretical anthropology*, 263).

2. The Comparative or Historical Method, here capitalized, refers to a procedure or conceptual apparatus employed throughout the eighteenth and later centuries in

foregoing analysis of the distributions of the two classes of dated cultural changes in certain European, North African, and Middle Eastern communities calls for something other than their description alone, or their submission to a generalization which recoils from the utilization of dated events. It calls for an explanation, a "theory," an "hypothesis," appropriate to *dated* similarities or regularities, suggesting how such *dated* similarities could have come about.

Of course, it would be fatuous to assume that uniformities observed in the antecedents of only two or three random collections of dated changes, such as the presses and the Christian congregations, could have permanent scientific meaning in themselves alone (though they accord in some respects with the results reached in several similar and earlier studies).[3] But the detection of such uniformities suggests that more inquiry along the same lines could helpfully be carried on.

Therefore, in the presence of the possibility that more extended study of other dated collections may show similar configurations, it seems wise to consider at once the form or forms an explanation of these phenomena might or should assume. Is it possible that classes of dated changes such as appear in the histories of the presses and the churches may have been preceded by similar classes of dated antecedents? Is it possible that the configurations of geographical spread may have been correlated with similar geographical antecedents? If so, in what form, model, or paradigm, should the discoverable elements of a hypothesis be stated? As historical "laws" or as historical "processes"? And what are the differences between a "law" and a "process"?

Anthropologists who read the literature on historical methodology will be aware of the long, and sometimes repetitious, argument as to the appropriateness of the use of the concept of natural law in dealing with historical uniformities. Recent debate on this question may be found in the works of Gardiner, Dray, Hempel, White, Hook and others,[4] usually under the rubric of "covering laws." The results

---

the construction of developmental, evolutionary, or progressive series of civilizations, cultures or institutions. It is to be sharply distinguished from the kinds of *comparison* advocated by social anthropologists, such as Evans-Pritchard, or historians, such as Marc Bloch. (See Kenneth Elliot Bock, "The comparative method of anthropology," 269–280; and *The acceptance of histories,* 122–130; John Wyon Burrow, *Evolution and society,* xi–xii, 10–14, 161–63, 228–33).

3. See Margaret T. Hodgen, "Glass and paper," 346–68; "Similarities and dated distributions," 445–67; *Change and history.*

4. Patrick Gardiner, *The nature of historical explanation;* William Dray, *Laws and explanation in history;* Carl Hempel, "The function of general laws in history"; Morton Gabriel White, "Historical explanation"; Sidney Hook, "A pragmatic criticism of the historico-genetic method"; and many others.

have been inconclusive. Although it is still traditionally assumed by some that the recurrences or regularities in nature, human and subhuman, are properly statable in terms of natural law, and although "laws" of history are still being "discovered" and vividly described by philosophers of history, other inquirers hold that the concept has no relevance for the historical studies; nor may it properly be utilized to refer to uniformities elicited as the result of the classification of like datable events, or the results of the comparison of classes of dated events.

Looking back briefly to assumed beginnings, one philosopher tells us that the idea of natural law arose from human cultural experience. It was conceived by Aristotle as a moral postulate for the evaluation of human conduct in the context of the political state, itself an historical and datable social institution.[5] Another philosopher takes a different view. "What Aristotle wanted, what all scientists and philsophers want," says George Boas, "is sentences (i.e. verbalizations) which will be true regardless of times and places, and consequently they have to find objects which are *non-temporal* and *non-spatial*" (Italics added).[6] In the long course of thought and controversy, although frequent efforts have been made to state the "laws of history," the earlier affiliation of the concept of natural law with the historical and the datable has been almost completely eroded. In modern scientific usage, the term "natural law" has come to mean a verbal statement of what happens uniformly if nothing interferes, or in abstraction from the eventful viewed as accidental.[7] Thus "natural law" is not a statement of uniformities derived from the classification or study of dated events. Natural laws are regarded as inherent in the nature of things separated conceptually from the dated, the accidental, or the contingent.

The need for these distinctions may be clarified, as suggested by Professor Teggart, by a short consideration of the study known as physiology. In the laboratory conduct of this form of inquiry the aim of the investigator "is to achieve a description of the functioning of the 'human body' by examination and comparison of a very large

5. "It only later acquired the modern scientific connotation of some positive uniformity in the sequence of natural phenomena" (Bidney, *Theoretical anthropology*, 12; see also Teggart, *Theory and processes*, 159).

6. George Boas, "Some assumptions of Aristotle," 24–35, note 5.

7. For the impact of this definition upon those who seek to deal with the temporal uniformities elicited in historical geology, see George Gaylord Simpson: "Laws are generalizaions . . . but . . . of a very special kind. They are complete abstractions from the individual case. They are not even concerned with what individuals have in common . . . [They are] abstracted entirely from contingent configurations" ("The historical factor in science," *in This view of life*, 126–27. See also Charles Coulston Gillispie, *Genesis and geology*, 121–48; Teggart, *Theory and processes*, 88, 90, 92, 133, 147, 159, 169).

number of human bodies. The description is given, however, without reference to any actual body" (at any specific place or date); "it represents the current conception of 'the way things work' in a 'normal,' 'abstract,' or 'ideal' human body." The results arrived at may well be "true," and useful. Someone may call them "laws," but they are nonhistorical; they are "timeless." On the statement of a natural law, so conceived and often achieved under laboratory conditions, what happens outside the laboratory, be it flood or fire, famine or social revolution, has no bearing. The laboratory statement is a verbal description of the way things work in a sheltered environment, if nothing is allowed to interfere with their working; "and natural science in general is concerned with the investigation of the way things work under laboratory conditions" in abstraction from dated intrusions.[8] It is this noninterference with working which is nonhistorical and which, since it conforms with the accepted concept of natural law, precludes the use of that concept as a description of any uniformity which may be or may have been elicited from the classification of similar dated historical events (or that which is regarded by logicians as accidental or contingent). Anthropologists, or other students of man, who seek to construct a universal, "natural" history of culture or society, or to elicit uniformities from human and dated history which they designate as "natural laws," are thus "simply not reckoning with the empirical facts of history,"[9] or with the idea of "natural law" as employed in the natural sciences.

The concept of process, on the other hand, is a more appropriate instrument in the hands of those who engage in the study of temporal or dated cultural phenomena; or who find themselves obliged, after effecting their classifications of dated events, to make some accounting for the regularities which emerge. According to its more formal definition, the word "process" refers to the existence of a temporal, repetitive, replicated, series of actions, operations, or motions, involved in the accomplishment of an end, either natural, artificial, or cultural. It is thus the preferred term when dated, or measurable,

8. Frederick John Teggart, "Notes on 'timeless' sociology, a discussion," 363; Simpson, *This view of life*, 122; Hodgen, "Distributions and processes," *in Change and history*, 97–124.

9. Bidney, *Theoretical anthropology*, 263. "Science makes suitable assumptions at the beginning of its process of thought; it impoverishes reality in order to get under way at all; it can proceed only by means of highly artificial manipulation of the residue of experience which it retains. Laws are . . . our accounts of Nature's doings or habits not hers. . . . The world of science is clipped to fit the laws" (Frederick Robert Tennant, "Natural law,"IX: 200). "To speak of the 'laws of history' is either to misunderstand the nature of history or to use 'laws' in an unacceptable sense" (Simpson, *This view of life*, 130; *Geography of evolution*, 58–59).

motion-in-time toward an end is implied; or, especially, when something is made, produced, or changed from one thing into another.[10] It is invoked more commonly in its artificial or technological sense for the description of the repetitive and temporal step-by-step procedures of manufacturing operations, such as the step-by-step series of operations in making sugar from sugar cane, in constructing motor cars on an assembly line, in shelling and canning green peas; or when human behavior shows a similar replicated series of actions.

However, just as technological or artificial processes should be perceived as different from one another and distinguished from natural processes, i.e. the process of making sugar from the process of digestion, so two types of *cultural* processes should be recognized. There are, first, recurring cultural activities, ceremonials, rituals, such as those associated with marriage, religious observances, or "the rites of passage," which when frequently repeated with each commonly experienced human need bestow the appearance of continuity and unity on all cultures, and among primitive peoples are from time to time observable and describable in some temporally limited "present."[11] There are, secondly, those similar series of cultural events, changes, or classes of event-marked cultural change, which are manifested over relatively longer periods of time; are terminated with similar results; and are recoverable, like the dated changes associated with the introductions of the printing presses or the Christian congregations, by historical investigation. Time, sequence and the replication of sequences are involved in all processes, but the time intervals between the elements of datable historical processes may often be long—very much longer than in technological processes.

In other words, users of the concept of "process" acknowledge at least three main types of uniform sequences of actions or events, differing from one another not only in their naturalness, artificiality, or historicity (and the several means by which their descriptions are obtained), but in the length of time consumed[12] by the step-by-step

10. Obviously in the study of events "it would tend to clarify thought if we were to employ the word 'process,' a term for the acutal operation described in place of the word 'law,' a term for the verbal description," and which excludes events (Teggart, *Theory and processes*, 164). *Social Sciences in historical study*, 96; R. C. Lewontin, "The concept of social evolution," V:202–210.

11. For the relation of this type of social process to the interests of the functionalists, see Marion J. Levy and Francesca M. Cancian, "Functional analysis," VI: 21–43 and also I: 321–22.

12. "Studying life from the historical point of view means giving attention to the element of time. All dynamic studies of life processes involve time. Processes produce changes and changes occur in time. (Even instantaneous changes have reference to *before* and *after*.) The time scale of many biological studies is severely restricted.

completion of each. For there is such a process as the step-by-step completion of digestion, which recurs frequently over short intervals of elapsed time, or may even be a continuous operation. These steps are recoverable for description by laboratory techniques and isolation from circumstances, events, and accidents occurring in the environment external to the laboratory. The resemblance here to a physiological "law," described below, is close.

Another group of "processes" is illustrated by the geological operation of erosion, or the sequential, repetitive, cultural activity already referred to as the "rites of passage." These processes may consume longer temporal intervals for their completion; they are not always continuously recurrent; and they are usually recoverable, not under laboratory conditions, but by field observation in the *present*. In eliciting processes such as these, the doctrine of uniformitarianism invoked by geologists and based upon the principle that the present is the key to the past, permits the inquirer, in the absence of datable fossil evidence to take the position that "earth history . . . can be explained in terms of natural forces still observable as acting today." A like argument is not unknown among anthropologists, who seek thus to recover the history of preliterate peoples; or by other students of social phenomena whose studies of current or present social activities are extrapolated as descriptions of the social past.[13]

A third group of processes, not deducible under laboratory conditions or from any regularities elicited from study in the present, is hopefully to be found in the analysis of the archives and raw materials of datable human history; and is already attained in the study of temporally

---

Reliable observations of living nature cover, at most, a few hundred years and are usually still more stringently limited. Laboratory experiments usually cover a few hours or days, at most a few years. The history of life involves a far longer time scale, the scale of geological time. The age of the earth is now known to be well over 3,000,000,000 years. . . . On this long time scale . . . we are studying mainly the results of processes that are exceedingly slow in terms of human life or experimentation. . . . There are . . . numerous essential factors of evolution that cannot be studied in the laboratory at all because they demand the longer-time scale" (Simpson, *Geography of evolution,* 3-4).

13. Of course, students of human activities who suggest that the short time results achieved in laboratories, in social surveys, in fleeting visits to primitive tribes, will yield knowledge of fundamental social processes, run the risk of emphasizing secular activities, or less significant short-term movements of cultural behavior, at the expense of ignorance of those typical of longer spans of time. As Professor Simpson says of the phenomena of long-term geological change: "There are always periods of higher and lower activity. High points may occur near the beginning, around the middle, near the end, near both beginning and end of the span, or in other patterns, but they are always there," ready to be elicited if the investigative procedure permits. (George Gaylord Simpson, *The meaning of evolution,* 105.) This is equally true of long-term human historical cultural phenomena.

arrangeable geological strata, and their enclosed fossilized documents. These processes of culture change, or of earth history, are consummated, if ever, only over relatively long, or very long, periods of past time. They may or may not have been recurrent. That remains to be seen. Their significance for the study of man and nature lies in their possible recovery by way of the classification of the dated events of human history, or the classification of the temporally arrangeable documentary materials of earth history.[14]

Of course, explanations of the distributions of the printing press and Christian congregations abound in the literature of each of these supremely important elements of western culture. It has been said, for example, that increased literacy[15] and easier access to supplies of paper[16] had much to do with providing a favorable environment for the establishment of the presses; while, in the minds of church historians, the formation of Christian groups is associated with many prior conditions: the Hellenizing of the East; the vast geographical extension of the Roman empire; the universalism of political philosophy; the breakup of the ancient world; the rising vogue of mystical religions; and the worldwide yearning for salvation from sin.[17]

But setting aside these more or less general and ad hoc interpretations for the moment, an examination of the local and common antecedents of the two early trait distributions, in the relatively few communities which actually accepted them, quickly sustains what many thoughtful students have already suspected, namely, the superior appropriateness in dated classes of cultural changes of the concept of process to the concept of natural law. For although the temporally and geographically arranged results, appearing in the foregoing tables and maps, reflect relatively short periods of time in the total dated record of each trait, and although they must therefore *be recognized as illustrations of method only*, these periods are longer than many widely

14. "*Geology is the subject which introduced a historical dimension into science.* . . . The geologist, like the historian, had to rely largely on interpreting the relics of change. He could neither experiment nor quantify " (Italics added. Charles Coulston Gillispie, *The edge of objectivity*, 291; Simpson, "The historical factor in science," in *This view of life*, 121–48; Teggart, *Theory and processes*, 159–67; John Herman Randall, Jr., *Nature and the historical experience*, 37–93; Paul Meadows, "The scientific use of historical data," 53–58.)

15. Henry Stanley Bennett, *English books and readers, 1475 to 1557*: 9–10, 19–29. See also, Curt Ferdinand Bühler, *The fifteenth century book*, 42–44; and Elizabeth L. Eisenstein, "The advent of printing and the problem of the Renaissance."

16. The Gutenberg Bible, printed on vellum, used up the skins of no less than 5,000 calves. Bühler, *Fifteenth century book*, 41–42.

17. Carl Gustav von Harnack, *The mission and expansion of Christianity in the first three centuries*, 19–23; Samuel Angus, *The religious quests of the Greco-Roman world*, 16–17, 19, 25, 93.

accepted as appropriate in contemporary social surveys, in which the past is interpreted as an extrapolation of the present, or in studies framed in terms of natural law. Moreover, these results in the form of distributions of sites of the two cultural changes are not statistical samples. They are stated with reference to the *totality of these classes of events for the dated periods under examination,* and consequently, if there be rhyme or reason in "history," their antecedent dated records should exhibit to the student of historical processes a number of common steps and conditions. Unlike flecks of pepper, shaken upon a sheet of paper, the distributions of mapped symbols, representing changing communities, are not random.

If the relative fewness of accepting communities, both early and late, be considered, and if the question of the uniformity of historical elements, events, steps, or conditions preceding acceptance be explored, it seems to be an inescapable conclusion that a common process of change may be at least partially observed and statable. Such a process exhibits at least three common steps, elements, or conditions. The first step in the establishment of the members of each class of these two dated changes, the class of presses and the class of congregations, is the unquestionable expression of individual initiative on the part of certain often namable and particular individuals. The second step, element, or condition in a possible common process is the appearance of this manifestation of individual initiative from among those who were alien or foreign to the communities which ultimately yielded acceptance to the change in question. The third is the assertion of foreign, individual initiative in an urban or trading environment within easy access to various means of contemporary communication.

In each of the two categories of dated cultural changes or distributions under consideration, beginning with the initiating acts of Jesus (a particular man) and Johann Gutenberg (a particular man), and followed thereafter by many other individual acts of cultural innovation, scholarship not only confirms the significant role of first donors in the process of cultural change, but also shows them to be nonresidents or migrants (known or named) into community cultures urban in character and located strategically on a network of ancient, much-traveled roads, rivers, or sea lanes.[18]

18. In *The Cambridge medieval history,* T. M. Lindsay speaks of "a system of magnificent roads for the most part passable all the year around, [which] united the capitals with the extremities from Britain and Spain on the west to the Euphrates on the east" (T. M. Lindsay, "The triumph of Christianity," I:88). See also Sir William Ramsay, "Roads and travel (NT)," *Dictionary of the Bible* Extra Volume 375–402; Michael Postan, "The trade of medieval Europe: the north," and Robert Sabatino

Turning, then, to the documentation of printing history, one finds that owing to the immense interest among bookmen in the collection of incunabula,[19] or the books published by movable metal type from 1450 to 1500, there is no dearth of the names[20] of the printers who set up the first presses, nor of the European towns or other localities in which their initiative was exercised. And the same is only a little less true for the founding of the earliest Christian groups. Not a stone has been left unturned, not a shred of evidence unexamined, which might yield information concerning the names of disciples, apostles, teachers, catechumens, or missionaries; the paths of their geographical wanderings; and the places in which they were successful in converting local groups to the doctrines they carried. If controversy continues in these two literatures as to names, dates, nationality, and movements of these two resolute bands of initiators, it is not because individuals had no part in the process of cultural change (or because cultural change should best be viewed as developmental or evolutionary, and therefore "natural" and inevitable) but because documentation here, as in all early historical inquiry, including the *science* of historical geology, is sometimes less full than might be desired.

Dealing first with the introduction of the printing presses during the last fifty years of the fifteenth century, an analysis of name, date,[21] and place material, afforded so generously to the student by the documentation of collectors of incunabula, shows quite clearly not only that German printers played a predominant role in the establishment of the first presses, but that many of them had received instruction in Mainz (in the master's workshop), or in shops already manned by Gutenberg-trained printers (see Chart 1). As shown in Table 3, wherever the printing press was first installed as a change from scribal copying, German or other nonresident printers were heavily represented in the founding of the presses in the decades of 1460-69 and 1470-79, in the former by 100%, in the latter by well over 50%.The same story is told again, and more graphically

---

Lopez, "The trade of medieval Europe: the south," II, 137-38, 150-51, 293, maps facing 138-40, and 299; Caroline A. J. Skeel, *Travel in the first century after Christ*, maps facing pp. 1 and 111.

19. Konrad Haebler, *The study of incunabula*, 7-37; Svend Dahl. *History of the book*, iii.

20. To mention only a few, Ulric Zell, Sensenschmidt, Sweinheym, Pannartz, Neumeister, Ruppel, de Spira, and Zainer. Approximately 30,000 incunabula have been preserved to the present time at least one copy each. (Haebler, *Study of incunabula*, 205.)

21. On dating of incunabula, see Haebler, *Study of incunabula*, 97, 104, 164-71.

Chart 1. Sites of First or Newly Established Presses Founded by German or Other Alien Printers from 1460–69 to 1470–79.

1460–69		1470–79	
		Naples	1471
		Speier	1471
Strasbourg	1460	Ulm	1473
		Wurzburg	1479
Bamberg	1461		
Foligno	1463		
Subiaco	1465		
		Messina	1478
Cologne	1466	Oxford	1478
		Siena	1479
Eltville	1467		
Rome	1467		
Augsburg	1468		
		Beromun-ster	1470
		Utrecht	1470
		Vienne	1473
Basel	1468	Vicenza	1474
		Sant' Orso	1474
		Modena	1475
		Milan	1471
		Trent	1475
Venice	1469	Toscolano	1478
		Pignerolo	1478
		Colle de Valdelsa	1479
		Florence	1471
		Mantua	1471
Nürnberg probably before	1470		

Presses founded by Germans known to have worked in Mainz 1457–79

Chart 1. (Continued)

1470–79

Presses founded by Germans	Paris	1470	German from Constance and Colmar
	Padua	1472	German from Prussia
	Saviligno	1473	German
	Alost	1473	German
	Valencia	1473	German probably
	Bruges	1474	German
	Louvain	1474	German
	Saragossa	1475	German
	Palermo	1476	German from Worms
	Tortosa	1477	German
	Seville	1477	German probably
	Larida	1479	German
Presses founded by aliens from other nations	Treviso	1471	Fleming from Ghent
	Genoa	1471	Printer from Antwerp
	Ferrara	1471	Printer from France
	Mondovi	1472	Printer from Antwerp
	Lyons	1473	Printer from Liege
	Buda	1473	Printer from Italy
	Turin	1474	Frenchman from Burgundy
	Westminster	1474	Printer from Bruges
	Piacenza	1475	Printer from Cremona
	Angers	1476	Frenchman from Paris

Table 3. The Number of Alien Printers Who Founded the Earliest Presses Compared with the Total Number of New Sites of Presses.

Dates	German Nationality	German or Other Aliens	Total Alien Printers	Total New Printing Sites
1457	1		1	1
1460–69	10		10	11
1470–79		42	42	77

in Chart 1, where it may be observed that printers from the first cluster (composed of Mainz, Eltville, Bamberg, Strasbourg, Augsburg, Cologne, and Basel)[22] or their apprentices have established many of the presses elsewhere, in Italy, France, and Spain, during the period from 1460 to 1479.[23]

Judging from the record of men employed at various times in Gutenberg's shop in Mainz, it would seem that the number of those who learned the art of printing directly from the master, or his immediate associates, was comparatively large.[24] At all events, in the decade of 1460–69, just after Gutenberg began his work in 1457, print shops were established in eleven new communities (Table 3). Six of these were near Mainz and show clearly as a geographical cluster (Map 1A). Of these four were started by printers who had worked in Mainz; while five others were established in Switzerland[25] (Basel) and Italy (Foligno, Subiaco, Rome, and Venice), all with similar German antecedents (Chart 1). That is to say, the presses at Basel and Foligno owe their existence to printers who came from Mainz, the remainder to other Germans.

In the decade from 1470–79 men of German origin still appear as founding printers in Italy, France, the Low Countries, and Spain, but to these were added a "second generation" of non-German craftsmen, many of whom nevertheless had worked in presses founded

---

22. *Catalogue of books printed in the XVth century now in the British Museum*, III: ix.

23. Here, as in Chart 1, the first two decades of the printing press are being subjected to closer analysis than the last two, though in these latter decades the same elements of individual initiative, often German, but more often by nonresident printers from other nations, still prevailed.

24. Bernard Alexander Uhlendorf, "The invention of printing and its spread until 1470," 200.

25. That Bertoldt Ruppel, the printer in question, was an employee of Gutenberg is stated by several sources: John Clyde Oswald, *A history of printing*, 142; Uhlendorf, "Invention of printing," 208; *Catalogue of books printed in the XVth century now in the British Museum*, II: 359; III: 713.)

by Germans or had migrated from the first clusters which were sites of presses founded by Germans to various communities in other European nations. Chart 1 shows many of these lines of technological descent among migrants.[26] In any event, from the standpoint of describing the initiating agent in the process of change resulting in the establishment of the printing press in many fifteenth-century communities, a correlation is close between Mainz as a training center, migrating printers from Mainz,[27] new presses, and the accepting communities which received them. Despite the fact that "embarking on the business of master printer was no light matter," dissatisfied workmen simply loaded their carts with their heavy equipment and moved on from town to town.[28]

It is not suggested here that the elements of this three-step process of change, expressed in the cultural acceptance of the printing press, is newly stated. Some may have been mentioned in the literature before. In this study, however, they have been arrived at by a new concept of the classifiability of like events with the results which flow from such classification and comparison.

Turning now to the records of the Christian church on the question of the first step in this process of religious changes, or the national origin of prime movers, every one knows that Christianity, like the Renaissance printing press, was started in a small way by individual believers. It was carried first by the unorganized enthusiasm of Jesus's immediate followers, later, by the more organized journeys of Paul and his associates, and later still, by word of mouth through a missionary "movement" composed of countless more or less anonymous teachers, catechumens, and preachers.[29]

It is instructive, and germane to the solution of the problem involved, to recall just how small[30] the earlier group of individual agents of this great religious change actually was, and how few were the earliest

26. There is much controversy in the literature over the names and provenance of founders. This study has leaned upon the *Catalogue of books printed in the XVth century now in the British Museum.*

27. Colin Clair, *A history of printing in Britain*, 13.

28. Strangely enough, apart from Germany, England was the only region in which the pioneer printer, Caxton, was a native; and Caxton is said to have learned the craft in either Cologne or Bruges, where German printers were at work in 1466 and 1477, respectively (Ibid., 7, 12, 13). "With the exception of Caxton, Thomas Hunt of Oxford, and possibly the anonymous printer of St. Albans, all the printers at work in England until 1513 appear to have come from abroad . . . [moreover] it would not be far from the mark to state that two thirds of all persons residing in England connected with the book trade from 1476 to 1535 were aliens" (Bennett, *English books and readers*, 30).

29. See pp. 57, 81, 82, 83, 87, 88, 91, 92, and 93 for a more detailed description of Christianization in Carthaginian North Africa.

30. As was also true of the introduction of the printing press.

efforts to proselytize.[31] Initiated by an individual man in Judea, Christianity, at the outset, was one of the smallest of the many cults which competed for the attention of the Greco-Roman world.[32] Its known membership, after Calvary, was composed of the original eleven[33] gathered around Simon bar Jonah, or Peter, augmented soon by a few others. Some of the later members of this little band were new believers, and some were those who had formerly been members of the personal following of Jesus but had been dispersed temporarily after the Crucifixion. According to the Book of Acts, the number of Christians during these earliest years reached about 120,[34] and they worshipped in a Jewish synagogue. By Pentecost, and the episode of glossolalia, their numbers had apparently increased to something like five hundred.[35]

According to Harnack,[36] this first small group, a sect within Judaism sometimes called the Nazarenes,[37] remained in Jerusalem for twelve years, although, of the original twelve followers of Jesus, only Peter, James, and John, receive mention again in Acts.[38] Gospel preaching, which began upon the fifty-first day after the Crucifixion, was at first directed to Jews by Jews, largely in Jerusalem. Soon individual followers, or congregations, began to find their way to other sites in Judea, Galilee, Samaria, or on the seacoasts of the eastern Mediterranean (Map B2). Here, and in Jerusalem, foreign Christians, such as the Libertini, the Cyrenians, Alexandrians, Hellenistic Jews, and others from Cilicia and Asia were either admitted to the original Nazarene synagogues, or joined together to form meeting places of their own (usually in homes) on the basis of nationality.[39]

After the stoning of Stephen, all Christians, except the apostles, were scattered abroad throughout the regions of Judea and Samaria,[40] where they continued to act as carriers of the new religion. A still

31. Apparently, Jesus "was but little concerned with organization" (Kenneth Scott Latourette, *A history of the expansion of Christianity*, I: 53).
32. Angus, *The religious quests*.
33. The number 12 was symbolic in Israel, so after the betrayal by Judas Iscariot it was necessary to choose another to take his place. The choice fell on Matthias. (Joseph Klausner, *From Jesus to Paul*, 169–70; *Interpreters Bible*, IX: 31. For names of the "twelve," see p. 58, note 29.
34. Klausner, *From Jesus to Paul*, 269–70; Acts I:15.
35. Ibid., 275. Acts II:41 mentions this increase but, according to Klausner, exaggerates it. The estimated size of the "church" in A.D. 250 over a century later was about 30,000. (Latourette, *A history of Christianity*, 95)
36. Harnack, *Mission and expansion*, 44–45, 45 n. i.
37. Latourette, *A history of Christianity*, I: 74; Harnack, *Mission and expansion*, 399 ff.
38. *Interpreters Bible*, IX: 31.
39. Harnack, *Mission and expansion*, 45, 46 n. 4, 49 n. 3.
40. Ibid., 51; Acts, VIII:1.

more decisive step was taken a little later at Antioch in Syria, where Jewish Christians, some of whom had also reached Phoenicia, Cyprus, and Crete, began to preach to the Greeks in that metropolitan city. Here, in Antioch, the first Christian community of any size outside Jerusalem was formed, and here also was founded the first pagan, Gentile, or Hellenistic Christian congregation.[41]

In other words, though Paul has become the most celebrated of the earliest carriers of Christianity to Asia Minor, Greece, Macedonia, Italy, and possibly Spain in the first century—regions in which, be it noted, he was a foreigner—he was by no means the first or only missionary in some of these Gentile areas.[42] It will be remembered that even on his first journey, begun at Antioch in Syria A.D. 43-45, he was accompanied by Barnabas and John Mark.[43]

As these three men went down to Seleucia in Syria, the first part of their sea voyage took them to the city of Salamis in Cyprus, where John Mark served as interpreter. Crossing the island to Paphos, they went on to Perga in Pamphilia, or "into the broad Greek world of Asia Minor." From Perga, Paul and Barnabas (without John Mark) went to Antioch in Pisidia, thence to Iconium in Laconia, to Derbe and Lystra (also in Laconia), back to the Pisidian Antioch and Perga, and finally by ship to their starting point, Antioch in Syria. In this first voyage of preaching and teaching, and even more so in the second and third,[44] which carried him finally to Rome, Paul had many fellow workers, companions, and even predecessors, who anticipated, confirmed or extended his own efforts.[45] Among those who may be named were Silas, Timothy, Luke, Aquila and Priscilla, and Apollos. No one will ever know the true number of these earliest carriers of Christianity. According to Harnack, they remain unnamable by

41. Harnack, *Mission and expansion*, 52; *Interpreters Bible*, IX: 88-91; Acts XI:19-22.

42. "Paul never claims in his letters to have been absolutely the pioneer of the Gentile mission" (Harnack, *Mission and expansion*, 48). In Rome "the gospel had already been preached, and a great church had been organized by unknown missionaries" (Ibid., 76).

43. "It would be very strange if Paul and Barnabas were the only leaders of missionary tours from Antioch, and if the only directions in which the Antiochene missionaries traveled in these thirty or forty years was west and northwest." It is reasonable to suppose that some went east, perhaps as far as Edessa (Urfa), "where a Jewish population provided a natural foothold" (Latourette, *A history of Christianity*, I: 80; see also Map B2 where both Edessa and Beit Zabde appear as sites of congregations on the Tigris and Euphrates rivers as early as the first century A.D. See Frederick van der Meer and Christine Mohrmann, *Atlas of the early Christian world*, 188, 191, and Map 1).

44. For the second and third voyages, see Klausner, *From Jesus to Paul*, 371-421.

45. "It seems a reasonable conjecture, that he [Paul] knew of other missionaries at work in the wide area of Palestine, southern and western Asia Minor, and the southern portions of the Balkan peninsula, and that he went only to those centers where they had not been." (Latourette, *A history of Christianity*, I: 82.)

modern students owing to contemporary uncertainty as to whether they should be known by their Semitic names, if Jewish, or whether non-Jewish workers should retain their pagan, worldly, mythological, Greek or Roman names.[46] The secret of Paul's success in introducing the new religion to the pagan world, says Harnack, lies therefore in the devoted effort of many named or unnamed *individuals.* Moreover, these carriers often found the ground already prepared for them by previous religious propaganda, or sometimes by actual missionary effort, carried on by alien Greeks or Jews, who had been Hellenized, or by a host of converts who stabilized many small congregations.

Thus, like the establishment of the printing presses over a thousand years later, these earliest Christian congregations (as well as countless others to be founded in succeeding centuries) *were not the outcome of some "natural" principle of cultural "growth" or evolution, operating in unsolvable mystery on the institutions of the local religions.* They were the demonstrably hard-won consequences of the personal effort of wandering, migrating, sometimes namable initiators. The evidence for this is overwhelming in the dated records of the first century. We read repeatedly in the New Testament, and later sources, of those who, without tangible organization or supportive public-relations machinery, made it their primary object in life to travel for longer or shorter periods from place to place proclaiming the Gospel.[47] Some tarried in a town for a day; others settled down for years, persuading and instructing neophytes, only then to move on to newer sites of initiating effort.

We know from accumulated evidence of many kinds that such efforts continued to be made by individual workers. But the names[48] of carriers of the Christian message, or definite records of their missionary labors still remain scarce for the three centuries following Paul's evangelization of the eastern Mediterranean. Little direct evidence, for example, bears on organized missionization by individual congregational groups, though it must have been carried on. There are few biographies of conversion.[49] Despite the presence in local church organizations of persons called bishops, apostles, prophets,

46. Harnack, *Mission and expansion*, 422–30. For a later period and the missionization of Northern Europe, see E. A. Thompson, "Christianity and the northern barbarians."
47. Latourette, *A history of Christianity*, I: 114–15.
48. Ibid., 86; Harnack, *Mission and expansion*, 485.
49. "Unfortunately, we know next to nothing of any details concerning the missionaries (apostles) and their labours during the second century." Their very names are lost with a few exceptions. Yet "the creation and career of this heroic order form of themselves a topic of supreme interest" (Harnack, *Mission and expansion*, 350–52).

and teachers, all of whom were engaged in a peripatetic ministry to their flocks,[50] it is Harnack's opinion that the most numerous and successful missionaries, during this period from A.D. 100 to A.D. 300 were anonymous individuals who from day to day confirmed their faith in the eyes of the pagans by their personal earnestness, readiness for sacrifice, and steadfastness.

Moreover, not only is it plain that Christian congregations were founded by nonresident individuals, Jewish aliens, or foreigners in the communities concerned, but also that such congregations were often themselves largely composed of nationless and displaced folk who, by the very fact of their alienation, were more disposed than acculturated natives to welcome new religious ideas and practices. Very important among these estranged and unassimilated peoples were many Jewish groups who resided in the communities of the Roman provinces; and, here, where there were Jews there were synagogues in which Christianity, a heresy of conservative Judaism, was taught openly or covertly.[51] In Acts XIV:1, we are told that at Iconium "they [Paul and Barnabas] . . . went into the synagogue and spoke in such a way that a great body of Jews and Greeks believed." At this time and later, there were colonies of Jews on the Black Sea; in Syria, Mesopotamia, Babylonia, and Media; in the African provinces of Mauritania, Numidia, and Byzacena;[52] in Gaul and Italy and Spain. Everywhere their numbers were impressive,[53] and in many of the pagan Greek and Roman communities, in which they had taken up their uneasy abodes, Christian congregations are known to have been formed. According to Klausner, Christianity was built up on the uprooted Judaism of the Diaspora.[54] The same was true in Carthaginian North Africa where urban areas ultimately became predominantly Christian, and agricultural serfs are said to have flocked to the new

50. Ibid., 342–68.
51. "And it came to pass in Iconium, that they went both together into the synagogue of the Jews, and so spake, that a great multitude both of the Jews and the Greeks believed" Acts XIV:1; Harnack, *Mission and expansion* 1, 15. See also Luigi Pareti, *History of mankind*, II: 870.
52. "We have evidence of Jewish communities in Carthage, Naro, Hadrumetum, Utica, Hippo, Simittu, Volubilis, Cirta, Auzia, Sitifis, Caesarea, Tipasa, and Oea, etc." (Harnack, *Mission and expansion*, 3 n. 2; Klausner, *From Jesus to Paul*, 7–40. See also Map D). According to Donaldson, North Africa also contained a marked fusion of aboriginal Libyans, indigenous Moors and Berbers, Phoenicians, Italians, and Greeks (Stuart A. Donaldson, *Church life and thought in A.D. 200*, 5–8). See also B. H. Warmington, *The North African provinces from Diocletian to the Vandal conquest*, 69–70, 73, 76–77.
53. Klausner, *From Jesus to Paul*, 32–34, 37, 42, 49.
54. Ibid., 49. See also E. Schürer, "Diaspora," Extra Volume 91–109. For the conversion of the northern barbarians, see E. A. Thompson, *in The conflict between paganism and Christianity in the fourth century*, 56–78.

faith when their Roman estate managers also made the transition. Many farms had their own Christian houses of worship; many villages, a bishop. In Hippo Regis, the home of Augustine, there were many Jews; in Carthage, their numbers were large.[55]

These rootless people and other exiles or depressed groups, who were non-Semitic but equally insecure, received with rejoicing the message that Jesus was the Messiah. Indeed, the transition from what has been called the early Jewish to a later Gentile mission has long been considered an episode freighted with far-reaching consequences. But the point to be made here is that however weighty the consequences, the conversion of the Gentiles, that is to say the transition from the polytheism of the classical world of Greece, Rome, North Africa, Egypt, and Spain, to the Judeo-Christian synthesis, was effected in only occasional communities during these earliest centuries, and by depressed, foreign or Jewish carriers.

To a mind made sensitive to the significance of the dated indices of cultural change, such as these, anything like the sweeping generalities of the social evolutionists, or even of the diffusionists of the age-and-area, botanical or seed-dispersion type, are not convincing. They fail to fit the plain historical facts.[56]

Were it not for the tenacity with which students of cultural change now and always have adhered to the paradigm of the biological analogy, interpreted as progress,[57] development, or social evolution (with its accompanying characterizations of universality, inevitability, gradualness, and continuity), it would be unnecessary to dwell upon these rather obvious elements in the dated or historical process of change of these two important traits. But whatever may be contemporary acceptance of traditional theories, the fact remains that along with the dated statements of the introduction of both the printing press and Christian doctrine go the names of individual carriers or innovators with the evidence of their migration from region to region. Neither the printing presses nor Christianity appeared spontaneously out of a prior technology or religious system without the active intercession of active innovators, alien individuals, or small disaffected human groupings. The names of these unusual men are given often

---

55. Frederik van der Meer: *Augustine the bishop*, 10, 19, 26–30, 78, 135.
56. Margaret T. Hodgen, "Geographical diffusion as a critierion of age," 346–47; John Christopher Willis, *Age and area*, v, 1, 6; Edward Sapir, *Time perspective in aboriginal American culture*, 25 ff.
57. Ludwig Edelstein, *The idea of progress in classical antiquity*; John Bagnall Bury, *The idea of progress*; Frederick John Teggart, *Theory and processes*; Teggart, *The idea of progress*; Teggart, "Spengler," *Saturday Review* 5: 597–98.

enough to make it clear not only that they were unlike their fellows, but that all must have had names even if many are now forgotten.

Nevertheless, when all the data sustaining the role played in the process of cultural change by the alien, depressed, wandering individual in it, it becomes evident that the process contained other steps or elements. It was not the alien alone who was responsible. It was his initiative, in combination with other probably indispensable elements, which culminated in the spreading acceptance of each trait. Comparison of the materials indicates the long-standing presence of assisting or channeling geographical conditions, of superior transportation systems, and except in North Africa, urban environments.[58]

Transportation on an "international scale" was available and widely used by cultural carriers both during the latter half of the fifteenth century in Europe, and in the Mediterranean basin during the first four centuries of the Christian era. This is not to say that every site of every printing press and every Christian congregation can be placed on a map of heavily traveled roads or that each trait was accepted only in the largest existing centers of population. But when this acknowledgment is made, when a comparison of the distribution maps of the presses and the congregations with contemporary means of travel, population figures, roads, and waterways is consulted, a connection seems to be indicated in better than a majority of cases.[59] Conversely, neither of these new culture traits was readily absorbed, during these earliest years, in rural or agricultural areas. A possible exception to this rule appears for Christian groups in the Carthaginian rural area of North Africa.

During the latter half of the fifteenth century, when movable metal type was first introduced into Renaissance Europe, trade and interregional intercourse was abundantly provided for by roads, navigable rivers, and sea lanes. Though the unkempt condition of the roads and a harsh winter climate often closed them to traffic for several months, there were always alternative sea routes or river lanes for

58. Insofar as changes in paleontological phenomena are concerned, Simpson speaks of the paths of faunal interchanges as "corridors, filters, and sweepstakes routes" (*Geography of evolution*, 87).

59. A generation after the discovery of the art of printing, "more than a score of German towns had printing shops. The fact that the majority were in western Germany is not only because the home of the art, Mainz, was in that part of the country, but also because it was here that the largest trade centers of the time were located, since the greater part of the trade went by way of the Mediterranean and the Levant. In general it was the large commercial centers that offered printers the greatest possibilities for continued activity, while in the small towns they found occupation for only brief periods" (Dahl, *History of the book*, 89).

long hauls or heavy commodities. Indeed, there seems to be no doubt that itinerant printers moved themselves and their novel equipment from older to newer sites with comparative and almost compulsive ease. Many moved more than once. During the first decade of distribution, as shown by thirteenth-century road maps, those who established the first cluster of presses around Mainz could choose between river or land routes. Indeed, lines of transcontinental traffic in Europe were so many as to defeat the drafting of a comprehensive map.[60] Mainz was not only on a much traveled road but also on the River Main. Bamberg lay a few miles due east on the Regnitz; Strasbourg, due south on the Rhine; and Cologne to the northwest on the same river. These four early printing communities were in frequent communication by road or water with other members of the first "German" cluster: Eltville, Augsburg, and Basel (Map A2). Ease of transport also prevailed among the members of the earliest Italian cluster—Foligno, Venice, Subiaco, and Rome. All were on land or water routes leading from Venice, over the Brenner Pass to Augsburg, Nürnberg, and other German cities. These towns, in turn, were linked by Ulm, Stuttgart, Würzburg, and Frankfort to that great western artery,[61] the River Rhine. Of the three clusters founded between 1470 and 1479 (Map A3), the most conspicuous is in northern Italy extending as far south as Rome. This geographical grouping is related not only to the River Po and an old road paralleling that river, but also to other roads connecting Venice with earlier German printing centers.

When the condition of the roads is recalled, says one student of incunabula, it is astonishing to learn

how much commerce there really was. Mainz had a large mercantile establishment by 1317; the fairs of its neighboring city, Frankfort, almost equaled in importance the great Flemish fairs. In truth, the merchant was the most important factor in German life of the Fifteenth Century, and it was not long before he was second only to the church as the best customer of the printer and the book trade. . . . The fact that the trade routes connecting the Italian and Flemish cities, and those between Nuremberg-Augsburg-Ulm and Lyons-Avignon crossed in the southwestern part of Germany must have had considerable bearing on the importance of Strasbourg and Basel as printing centers.[62]

60. Postan, "Trade of medieval Europe: the north," and Lopez, "The trade of medieval Europe: the south, II: Map 6 facing page 8, and 137–38, 140, 150–51, 291, 293; Robert Sabatino Lopez: *The birth of Europe* 298–301, see Map 20, on p. 299; Oswald, *A history of printing*, 35–36.
61. J. H. Parry, "Transport and trade routes," IV: 185.
62. Uhlendorf, "Invention of printing," 181–83.

The classification and mapping of the dated introductions of printing presses in the second decade of the last half of the fifteenth century, or from 1470 to 1479 (Map A3), thus not only indicate an increase in the numbers of the first German cluster around Mainz, they add a few other clusters. One of these was in the Low Countries, another in Italy. The former was obviously well served by sea lanes, roads, and rivers; the latter, composed of an unprecedented number of new members, lay on the River Po, or on ancient roads such as the Via Flaminia, the Via Aemilia, or the Via Aurelia[63] (Map A3). The same also seems to be true for those presses "disseminated at a distance" in France and Spain during the same decade. Their locations are rationalized by the presence of roads or other means of communication.

To be sure, travel was not rapid in the fifteenth century. Indeed, a hundred years later, it was still a nineteen-day trip from Milan to Venice by river boat. Nor was the land route over the Alps any faster. But slow and rough though they were, these routes served to facilitate the migrations of printers. Many of these craftsmen were Germans, to whom must be attributed the installation of Italian presses during this and earlier decades in Naples, Messina, Siena, Vincenza, Sant 'Orse, Modena, Mantua, Florence, Palermo, Tortosa, Genoa, Ferrara, Mondovi, Turin, Piacenza, Milan, Tuscolano, Pignolo, and Colle Valdessa. All were established by printers from Venice, who were themselves typographical descendants of the printers of Mainz (see Chart 1). Increased traffic and innovation is thus often said to be due to that great turning point in European economic history, the commercial revolution in Italy in the High Middle Ages. By the twelfth century, "Venice, Genoa, and other mercantile cities had surpassed in wealth the greatest business centres of the classic world. . . . In this, Italy was to the medieval economic process what England was to the modern."[64]

However, though good transportation may have played an important part in this economic resurgence, it should not be thought of as having "caused" the dissemination of the use of movable type, nor even to have formed a determining element in that process of cultural change. Since a "process" is to be defined as a temporal and repetitive series of actions toward the accomplishment of a repetitive end, the presence of highways was merely one element in the process, or better, a fostering condition.

63. Skeel, *Travel in the first century*, map facing p. 1; Lopez, "Trade of medieval Europe: the south" *Cambridge Economic History*, II, 290.
64. Lopez, "Trade of medieval Europe," II: 289-91.

In the process of religious change in the first century, or the establishment of Christian congregations by alien founders, transportation and trade seem to have operated in a similar way. In other words, three things are noteworthy in the early history of the church. One is the rapidity with which groups of recruits, believers, or congregations, were formed over wide areas; another is the constant intercourse among them, or their close supervision by traveling counselors; and, third, is the dependence of foreign founders and supervisors upon access to roads and waterways.

Within thirty short years after Calvary, Christian doctrine was being taught in groups not only in Palestine but also in Asia Minor, Macedonia, Achaia, Illyricum,[65] and even in Rome itself.[66] Converted in early manhood on the way to Damascus in the eastern Mediterranean, Paul in his old age could reasonably look forward to a missionary journey to the far west in Spain. The first epistle of Peter shows the same broad geographical horizon, this time in the Far East. Addressed to Jewish exiles of the Diaspora in the Asian provinces of Pontus, Galatia, Cappadocia, and Bithynia (all provinces in Asia Minor), the letter refers to a sister church in Babylon on the Euphrates.[67] These few facts, out of the many which could be assembled, reveal that at this early date the means of travel over the Mediterranean area had already reached a high stage of development. Any man, so minded, could move from the coast of the Atlantic to the Tigris and Euphrates, or even far beyond, with the stream of commerce.[68] Not only that, but the location of trade routes and the sites of the changes in local religious practices brought about by Jewish or other carriers show a clear concurrence with one another. The maps exhibiting the distributions and clusterings of Christian congregations in the first and second centuries coincide, not with rural areas, or areas unpenetrated by well-worn routes of travel (Map C),[69] but with a network of ancient well-traveled highways. The same is only a little less true in the third century, when to this concurrence is added the rather

65. Harnack suggests that the rate and range of this spread might have been due to the certainty that the world was soon to end (Harnack, *Mission and expansion*, 73–74).

66. In Rome, "the gospel had already been preached and a great church had been organized by unknown missionaries," before Paul reached the city (Ibid., 76).

67. I Peter I:1, 5:13.

68. Arnold Hugh Martin Jones, *The later Roman Empire*, II: 830–34; Skeel, *Travel in the first century*, 1–2. See also the maps in Carl Gustav Adolph von Harnack, *Die mission und ausbreitung des Christentums in den ersten drei jahrhunderten . . . Zweite neu durch gearbitete auflage . . . Mit elf karten*, 2 Bde. (Leipzig, 1906); Ramsay, "Roads and travel (in NT)."

69. See Map of *Chief Routes of the Roman Empire*, in Sir William Ramsay "Roads and Travel (in NT)"; Hastings *Dictionary of the Bible* (1923), Extra Volume, 384.

Map C. Roman roads in Asia Minor in the first century together with some other routes also traveled by Paul. (Modified from maps in *Travel in the First Century After Christ,* by Caroline A. J. Skeel, Cambridge University Press)

Roman _____

Pauline . . . . . .

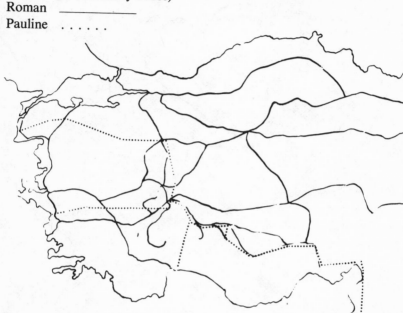

sudden appearance of the well-marked cluster in what is now Tunisian North Africa (Map B3). Undoubtedly, this dense localized distribution, though largely rural in setting, was subject to the urban influence of Carthage, the second commercial city in the western empire.[70] At the same time, most of the members of the distribution lie in close juxtaposition to the tributaries of the small Mallegue River system, or are situated on coastal highways and a network of interior roads (Map B3 and Map D).[71] Similarly, in the sparsely settled Roman

70. There were not only more than 100 African bishops by A.D. 256 ("Africa," I: 311), but from "Carthage and the other great coast cities of Africa and Numidia, such as Leptus, Hadrumetum, and Hippo Regius, roads converged on Theveste," and eastward from Carthage was a road "past the Syrtes and to Alexandria" (Skeel, *Travel in the first century,* 29-30) "From Carthage radiated the network of roads, traces of which survive after more than 1000 years of Mussulman rule" (Donaldson, *Church life,* 2).

71. The discrepancy between the number of church sites shown in North Africa on Map B3 and the van der Meer-Mohrmann Map 22 arises from the fact that the former includes only those new sites to which dates of founding may be assigned from A.D. 100 to 199, while the latter includes only those known to exist which sent bishops to the Synod of Carthage in A.D. 256.

Map D. The Diocese of Africa in A.D. 256 with some Christian churches and roads. (With permission of Elsevier, from *Atlas of the Early Christian World*/Nelson)

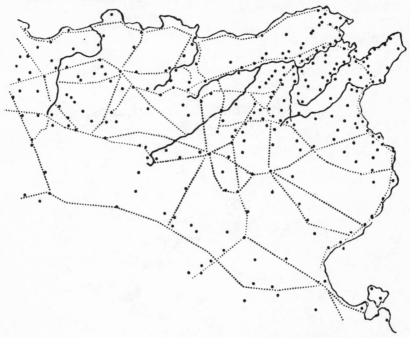

provinces of Germania, Belgica, Gallia, and Hispania the same regional concurrence between routes of travel and sites of religious change prevails.

It is not true, of course, that the process of change leading to the acceptance of movable type or the establishment of Christian groups *always* took place on roads or waterways, or on *all* roads or waterways. This is brought out forcibly by Sir William Ramsay in his essay on "Roads and travel (in NT)" in Hasting's *Dictionary of the Bible*. The new religion

was carried by ship to the Bythynian and Pontic harbours, and thence spread south into the northern and northeastern regions of the province of Galatia, including inner Pontus and the north of Cappadocia. Thus we find that this new thought and teaching, 'floating free on the currents of communication across the Empire' spread directly along the great tracks that led to Rome . . . and from that centre was redirected to the outlying parts of the Empire. As Christianity spread from Syria and Cilicia through the Cilician Gates, it did *not radiate out* west and north and northeast, but passed along the great route that led by Ephesus, Corinth and the sea-way, by Troas and Phillippi and the overland way, to Italy.[72] (Italics added)

When Paul and other carriers of the Gospel confined their work to the Roman world they were not only acting in the spirit of their times but also were breaking ground, guided by the practical possibilities of contemporary communication and travel. A little more than twenty years after Paul's death other routes began to be followed. Chrysostom extended his travels through South Russia and Hungary, to the upper Danube and the new province of Dacia. Indeed, travel, either for pleasure or business, under the Empire was performed with an indifference and confidence not to be repeated until the resurgence of economic activity in the Middle Ages.[73]

But this did not mean that the process of change leading to the formation of Christian groups, or the later founding of printing presses, took place everywhere on every road. Roads made innovations possible. They did not eliminate the central importance of individual choice of sites on existing means of transportation. The location and accessibility of means of transport are correlated with the geographical locations of cultural innovations merely in the sense that where roads or other means of travel existed, there also at some specific sites innovators made their appearance. Where, on the other hand, means of transport were absent, there cultural changes and innovators were also absent or infrequent.

A third and unmistakable element in the process of change which resulted in the distribution of these two new culture traits, as shown on the several maps, was the urban character of the settlements in which innovating and alien carriers chose to implant their new techniques or doctrines. This is not to say, of course, that the modern concept of the "city" may be extrapolated and applied, without modification, on the distributions of the sites of Renaissance printing presses or Christian groups. Such conceptual legerdemain would be fatal to a clear idea of what actually happened, or of this intrinsic feature of the process of cultural change. For "urban" communities in these earlier historical periods were both like and unlike some modern cities. They were like cities of today (though to a lesser degree) in that they were centers of trade and commerce. They were unlike them in size, or numbers of inhabitants.

72. Ramsay, "Roads and travel (in NT)," 383, column A.
73. Ibid., 397, column B.

Even though estimates are hard to come by, and must always be treated with caution,[74] and even though the Renaissance population of Europe as a whole was on the increase during the very decades of the introduction of the printing press, the total number of residents in what are often called the "cities" of the period was relatively small. It is known, for example,

that apart from Constantinople, that unique relic of the ancient world, no more than four or five European cities—Paris, Naples, Genoa, Venice, and possibly Milan—had reached . . . a population figure of 100,000 on the eve of the modern era. Only a handful—Florence, Bologna, Seville, Cordoba, Granada, Lisbon, and Ghent—are known, or may be assumed, to have numbered 50,000 or a little more. Upwards of a dozen other 'large' cities of late medieval times, among them Verona, Palermo, Rome, Messina, London, Barcelona, Cologne, Antwerp, Brussels, and possibly also Vienna and Prague, ranged from 30,000 to 50,000 inhabitants. Outside of Italy, Spain, and the Low Countries, even relatively important centres of international trade and industry, such as Toulouse, Strasbourg, Lübeck, Nürnberg, Augsburg, Danzig, and Ulm, barely reached, or did not exceed, a population of 20,000.[75]

It follows therefore that many of the sites of the earliest presses, though "urban," were relatively small as compared with modern large agglomerations of people.[76] What characterized them, or conferred their urbanity, was their participation in international trade. Many "drew their food from distant areas, exported their wares in all directions of the compass, played host to colonies of business men from other towns. . . . It was not the number of their inhabitants but their spirit which made the difference."[77] And this entrepreneurial drive came to be expressed in the plurality of printing presses introduced into some towns. Between 1469 and 1501, as has already been mentioned, Venice boasted of nearly 150 separate printing firms, or the establishment of an average of nearly five new presses a year.[78] That many succumbed to bankruptcy failed to deter the foundation of others in the same kind of urban atmosphere elsewhere.

As for Christian congregations, nearly all students of the process of acceptance of this new religion agree in regarding it also as a

74. Josiah Cox Russell, *Late ancient and medieval population,* 5-13.
75. Karl F. Helleiner, "The population of Europe from the Black Death to the eve of the vital revolution," IV: 81-82.
76. For a discussion of the population of printing centers, see Uhlendorf, "Invention of printing, 181-82; Curt Ferdinand Bühler, *The fifteenth century book,* 56, 145 n. 121; Russell, *Ancient and medieval population,* 47, 60, 61.
77. Lopez, "Trade of medieval Europe: the south," *Cambridge Economic History of Europe,* II, 300.
78. Bühler, *The fifteenth century book,* 54-55.

phenomenon of the city. We are told that within a generation after the death of Jesus, Christianity became part of the urban life of the Hellenistic world. As late as the fourth century, it was still an urban religion. This was due in part to the methods by which doctrines were diffused. The early followers of Jesus moved from "city to city," rapidly spreading the gospel over wider and wider territory, but at the expense of leaving the intervening countryside untouched. The early "churches" were thus in the "cities" and tended to remain so, except for North Africa and Egypt.[79] Here in Tunisia, a rural, populous, fertile, corn-growing region, Christianity made rapid strides by means of meetings in private homes or burial clubs,[80] more often than not in farming communities,[81] but under the influence of the city of Carthage.

In linking the process of cultural change with urbanism, in this study of two classes of dated changes, it should be remembered, however, not only that the actual number of persons in these centers was smaller than in the cities of today, but also that that number has to be estimated rather than accurately determined. One reason for this fact, and one particularly relevant to the forming of judgments concerning the distributions of Christian congregations, was the attitude of Roman administrators to census taking. Statistical topics now included in the study of population phenomena were then of little interest. Consequently, the estimates occasionally suggested by contemporary Latin writers were usually guesses without sound foundations.[82] Present-day difficulties in estimating ancient urban populations in the Empire have been increased by the fact that a "city," according to Roman custom, was a spatial unit different from the modern city. The Roman empire was a "mosaic" of "cities," but each urban unit was an administrative one including an economic and social center plus the inhabitants of what might well have been an extensive rural

79. The slow progress of Christianity in rural areas is attributed to the inherent conservatism of the peasantry, and the fact that they spoke local dialects rather than the two dominant tongues of city life, Greek and Latin (Arnold Hugh Martin Jones, "The social background of the struggle between paganism and Christianity," 17-19). "Christianity gradually conquered the countryside, it is true, but it was a very slow process, by no means complete even in the sixth century" (Ibid., 23).
80. Donaldson, *Church life,* 1-20.
81. Olive oil was produced in enormous quantities in "places which today are desert." Archaeological evidence from Tripolitania, Numidia, and Mauritania Sitifensis points to the middle of the third century as the time when villages began to expand and prosper." (See Maps B2, B3, B4, for the distribution of Christian groups.) "Africa supplied the world with oil almost alone." Even though countrymen, these farmers, with middlemen and merchants, were at this time the "pivot of the whole of the Mediterranean area" (W. H. C. Frend, "North Africa and Europe in the early middle ages," 67-68).
82. Russell, *Late ancient and medieval population,* 5.

area. Thus the population of some "cities" was small and sparse, but their territories were large. Conversely, others were densely populated within narrow rural borders.[83]

Historians who attempt to estimate the population of the empire as a whole now assert that "it was and always has been small by modern standards"; while that of the cities, even the greater ones, was much less than usually imagined. The inhabitants of the city of Rome, for example, in the early fourth century, numbered merely one-half to three-quarters of a million; while Constantinople was about the same size in the sixth century. Alexandria, the third city of the empire, was about half the size of Constantinople; while Antioch in Syria, with about 150,000 to 200,000, led a list of many other important but much smaller communities.[84] Among these were some of the urban areas entered by Christianity in North Africa. Carthage, where Latin Christianity early appeared, and which enjoyed the same primacy on the African continent as Antioch in Syria, is estimated to have been composed of only 38,000 to 50,000 souls.[85] All of the other Christianized communities in the African provinces, such as Numidia, Byzacena, and Mauritania, were even smaller, containing from 2,000 to 20,000 souls. In Asia Minor and Greece innovating communities were also small. Smyrna and Ephesus could boast of but 90,000 and 50,000 respectively, while the population of Athens and Corinth was 50,000 and 28,000.[86]

These urban, and nearly always commercial, units, however, were the first human settlements to offer hospitality to the new religion. It is therefore an easy, if not compulsory, generalization to say that Christianity, like the printing press, followed the roads which carried trade and commerce, and stopped in the cities, and that urbanity of environment seemed nearly always to be an essential element to Christianizing change. Moreover, most audiences, addressed by missionaries or other spokesmen, were composed of persons with whom traders and merchants were in frequent contact. Since the Roman empire formed a vast market, the steady stream of professional recruiters for the new religion was paralleled by, or mingled with, a like stream of merchant sympathizers, many of whom either carried news of the existence of the new faith, or strove actively to impart its promises to fellow traders and customers. It was no "accident"

83. Jones, *Later Roman Empire*, I: 712–14.
84. Ibid., II: 1040.
85. Russell, *Ancient and medieval population*, 76, Table 79.
86. Ibid., 77, 80, Table 80, 83.

in the historiographical sense, that Paul was born in Tarsus with its linen weavers, and its border geographical position between east and west. This position gave to the old city not only sea routes to Phoenicia, Greece, Egypt, and other African, Spanish or western ports but also roads leading through the passes of Cilicia to Lycaonia and Galatia to the north and west, and eastward into Mesopotamia.[87] Like the peripatetic printers of the Renaissance, carriers of the new religion were foreigners to the people among whom they found themselves, some of whom were Jews.[88] Paul's efforts, on his second journey, were often centered on cities in which there were Jewish colonies containing synagogues from which the faith could be spread to outlying districts. Later Jewish merchants, as well as pagan traders of many cultures, became carriers to Jewish as well as pagan sympathizers. In the Diaspora there was no national soil, no uninterrupted Hebrew tradition, no complete and consolidated Judaism. It was relatively easy, therefore, to alienate further the already alienated.[89]

87. Klausner, *From Jesus to Paul*, 306; Jones, *Later Roman Empire*, II: 848, 857; Latourette, *A history of Christianity*, I: 73, 75, 110.
88. For a discussion of Jews in Carthage, see Donaldson, *Church life*, 25-29.
89. Latourette, *A history of Christianity*, I: 41, 166; Klausner, *From Jesus to Paul* 29-30; for the number of Jews in Palestine and the Diaspora, see Ibid., 32-34; for merchants, see Jones, *Later Roman empire*, II: 865-72. "One has the impression that long-distance trade was increasingly in the hands of small minorities of Syrians and Jews" (Arnaldo Momigliano, "Christianity and the decline of the Roman empire," 8; on the Diaspora, see Pareti, *History of mankind*, 332-33, 521-25; E. Schürer, "Diaspora," 91-109. For a slightly different point of view, see Harnack, *Mission and expansion*, 44-72.

CHAPTER 6

In Closing

If the foregoing dated facts and arguments have been set forth with sufficient clarity, it should be unnecessary to emphasize again the intellectual gains to be won by unifying the study of man, or by dissolving for at least some inquirers the traditional disciplinary separation between anthropology and history. As for the historians, upheld by their long-time and dignified alliance with literature and its narrative devices, many may well prefer to persevere in the course followed by distinguished forebears, and this to the delight of a legion of readers. Many anthropologists, in this heyday of their popularity, may also feel that their customary ways of working have stood the test of time. They, too, may prefer, and find it professionally advantageous, to adhere to old questions and answers.

But whatever the reaction of the members of the company of historians to departures from narrative practice, and however stoutly anthropologists may cling to older paradigms, their situation vis-à-vis the on-going and rapid westernization of every corner of the world is critical. Though many elements of contemporary anthropological problems and methods of solution should not be abandoned, their objects of interest, the cultures of primitive or preliterate peoples, are undergoing changes which promise their rapid extinction, until they take their places with the dodo and dinosaur. Only too soon, face-to-face observation of this category of cultures, as living behavioral entities, will no longer be possible.

Meanwhile where is the more farsighted anthropologist to turn, with all of his expertise in cultural morphology, description, analysis, and comparison, and especially with his persistent interest in the solution of the problem of cultural change? To sociology, so neighborly and engulfing? There are many reasons for fearing that the habitual avoidance in the latter discipline of rigorous historical inquiry would mean for the anthropologist a relaxation in his particular and important cultural problems, and a loss of many of his long practiced skills. As has been said by Bidney, quoting Maitland, "anthropologists and sociologists who are seeking for a universal natural history of society and culture . . . simply are not reckoning with the empirical facts of history."[1]

The anthropologist may decide to remain within his accustomed metes and bounds and to continue his study of cultural change among the rapidly changing cultures of the preliterates whom he knows so well. In this case, he may infer, according to a current vogue, that findings made in the present of on-going cultural changes are acceptable as true, without historical check, without parallel checks with the dated changes of the past. Or again, when confronted with the problem of change among changing primitive folk, and the civilized as well, he may resort to evolutionary theory, finding the contemporary rapidity of changes in some traits part of the inevitable realization of civilization among all men. Or finally more hopefully, he may acknowledge that since what the anthropologists call "culture" is a common possession of all human groups, historical and nonhistorical, the study of change may best be conducted by the collection of dated changes, and turn his attention to the historical peoples.

Of course, the comparisons in this paper of only two classes of dated changes, the presses and the Christian congregations, are hardly enough to arrive at firm judgments as to the several steps in a generally stated process of cultural change. Nor is the event-and-change producing individual, with accompanying suggested conditions, an unheralded discovery. In varying contexts similar conclusions have been expressed before. In the context of dated cultural history and dated events, it merely calls attention to a promising new field of inquiry for anthropologists, just as an older field is fading away. As botanists have not reached judgments on the investigation of one or two families of flora, so anthropologists, or even historians, may well sharpen their insight into the process of historical and nonhistorical changes by pushing the collection of dated trait innovations.

As has been said before in a previous paper on the same subject, the questions a science puts, the concepts employed in the statement of its problem and solution, are a measure of its development. Only repeated exploration in the classification and arrangement of the dated events of cultural changes can suggest additional questions, the

1. David Bidney, Theoretical anthropology, 263.

formulation of new answers, or the refinement of old ones. Fortunately, there is no dearth of material, and the task of bringing it into eloquent order is no greater than that which has confronted students of processes in the natural world of geology, botany, and zoology.

What distinguishes the scientific attitude from its opposite, the unscientific, is not the failure of the latter to get acceptable results, but the willingness of the former to recognize that when acceptable results cannot be achieved in one way, there are still others open for trial.

That which unifies the disciplines of anthropology and history is their like belief in the explanatory function of the recovered past, and their attempts, though unlike, to recover it. What impedes unification, or closer cooperation, are unexamined and different procedures for that recovery, especially as these differences take cultural changes as a problem, accept developmental reconstructions of the past, and assert the uniqueness and unclassifiability of dated events.

Works Cited

Adeney, Walter Frederick. *The Greek and eastern churches.* Edinburgh: T. and T. Clark, 1928.

"Africa," *Encyclopedia Britannica* I: 311-312. Chicago: Benton, 1967.

Anderson, Robert T. "Anthropology and history," *Bucknell Review* 15 (1967): 1-8.

Angus, Samuel. *The religious quests of the Greco-Roman world: a study in the historical background of early Christianity.* London: Murray, 1929.

Bagley, Philip. *Culture and history: prolegomena to the study of civilizations.* New York: Longmans, 1958.

Barnett, Homer Garner. *Innovation: the basis of cultural change.* New York:McGraw-Hill, 1953.

Baumann, Hermann. "Fritz Graebner," In *The International encyclopedia of the social sciences.* Edited by David L. Sills, VI: 240-41. New York: Macmillan, 1968.

Beard, Charles Austin. "Written history as an act of faith," *American Historical Review* 39 (1934):219-231.

Becker, Carl Lotus. *Everyman his own historian.* New York: Crofts, 1935.

Bennett, Henry Stanley. *English books and readers, 1475 to 1557: being a study in the history of the book trade from Caxton to the incorporation of the stationers company.* Cambridge: Cambridge University Press, 1952.

Bennett, John William and Wolff, Kurt Heinrich. "Towards communication between sociology and anthropology," In *Current anthropology; a supplement to Anthropology Today.* Edited by William L. Thomas, Jr., pp. 329-51. Chicago: University of Chicago Press, 1956.

Berlin, Isaiah. "History and theory: the concept of scientific history," *History and Theory* (1960) I:1-29.

Bidney, David. *Theoretical anthropology.* New York: Columbia University Press, 1953.

Bloch, Marc. *The historian's craft.* New York: Knopf, 1953.

Boas, George. "The living book," *Library Journal* 76 (1951): 1972-5.

_____. "Some assumptions of Aristotle," Transactions of the American Philosophical Society, n.s. XLIX (1959): 1-98.

Bock, Kenneth Elliot. *The acceptance of histories: toward a perspective for social science.* Universtiy of California Publications in Sociology and Social Institutions III. Berkeley: University of California Press, 1956.

Bock, Kenneth Elliot. "Evolution, function, and change," *American Sociological Review* V (1963): 229-37.

_____. "The comparative method of anthropology," *Comparative Studies of Society and History* 8 (1965-66): 269-280.

Brinton, Crane. *Anatomy of revolution.* New York: Thorton, 1938.

British Association for the Advancement of Science. *Report of the 11th Meeting held at Plymouth July 1841.* London: John Murray, 1942.

Bühler, Curt Ferdinand. *The fifteenth century book: the scribes, printers, the decorators.* Philadelphia: University of Pennsylvania Press, 1960.

Burrow, John Wyon, *Evolution and society.* Cambridge: Cambridge University Press, 1966.

Bury, John Bagnall. *The idea of progress: an inquiry into its origin and growth.* London: Macmillan, 1920.

Carr, Edward Hallett. *What is history?* London: Macmillan, 1962.

Catalogue of books printed in the XVth century now in the British Museum. 9 volumes. London: Longmans, 1908-62.

Challener, Richard D. and Lee, Jr., Maurice. "History and the social sciences: the problem of communications. Notes on a conference held by the Social Science Research Council," *American Historical Review* 61 (1956):331-38.

Clair, Colin, *A history of printing in Britain.* London: Cassell, 1965.

Claudin, Anatole. *Les origines de l'imprimerie en France. Premiers essais a' Avignon en 1444.* Paris: Librairie A. Claudin, 1898.

Cohn, Bernard S. "Ethnohistory," In *International encyclopedia of the social sciences.* Edited by David L. Sills, pp. 440-48. New York: Macmillan, 1968.

Cosenza, Mario Emilio. *Biographical and bibliographical dictionary of the Italian printers and of foreign printers in Italy from the introduction of the art of printing into Italy to 1800.* Boston: G. K. Hall, 1968.

Cotton Henry. *A typographical gazetteer, attempted by the Reverend Henry Cotton . . . 2d edition corrected and much enlarged.* Oxford: Oxford University Press, 1831.

_____. *A typographical gazetteer.* 2d Series. Oxford: Clarendon Press, 1866.

Cultural patterns and technical change. From the Tensions and Technology Series. A manual prepared for the World Federation for Mental Health and edited by Margaret Mead. Reprinted as a Mentor Book by arrangement with the United Nations Educational, Scientific and Cultural Organization. New York: The New American Library of World Literature, 1955.

Dahl, Svend. *History of the book.* New York: Scarecrow Press, 1958.

Darwin, Charles. *The origin of species.* London: John Murray, 1959.

Dewey, John. *Logic.* New York: Holt, 1938.

"Diffusion," In *International encyclopedia of the social sciences.* Edited by David L. Sills, IV: 169-185. New York: Macmillan, 1968.

Dixon, Roland B. *The building of cultures.* New York: Scribner, 1928.

Donaldson, Stuart A. *Church life and thought in A.D. 200.* Cambridge: Cambridge University Press, 1909.

Dray, William. *Laws and explanation in history.* Oxford: Oxford University Press, 1960.

Edelstein, Ludwig. *The idea of progress in classical antiquity.* Baltimore: Johns Hopkins University Press, 1968.

Eggan, Fred. "Social anthropology and the method of controled comparison." In *Readings in cross-cultural methodology*. Edited by Frank W. Moore, pp. 101–128. New Haven: HRAF Press, 1961.

Eisenstein, Elizabeth L. "The advent of printing and the problem of the Renaissance," *Past and Present, a journal of scientific history* 45 (1969):19–89.

Ely, Richard G. "Mandelbaum on historical narrative: a discussion," *History and theory: studies in the philosophy of history* VIII (1969):275–299.

Evans-Pritchard, Edward Evan. *Anthropology and history*. Manchester: Manchester University Press, 1961.

_____. *Social anthropology: past and present*. London: Cohen and West, 1951.

Fenton, William Nelson. "Fieldwork, museum studies, and ethnohistorical research," *Ethnohistory* 13 (1966):71–85.

_____. "The training of historical ethnologists in America," *American Anthropologist* 54 (1952):328–339.

Firth, Raymond. "Function," In *Current anthropology: a supplement to anthropology today:* Edited by William I. Thomas, Jr., pp. 237–258. Chicago: University of Chicago Press, 1956.

_____. "Social anthropology," In *International encyclopedia of the social sciences*. Edited by David L. Sills, I: 320–324. New York: Macmillan, 1968.

Frend, W. H. C. "North Africa and Europe in the early middle ages," In *Transactions of the Royal Historical Society*, Fifth Series 5 (1955):61–80.

Fürer-Haimendorf, Christoph von. "Culture history and cultural development," In *Current anthropology: a supplement to Anthropology Today*. Edited by William L. Thomas, Jr. Chicago: University of Chicago Press, 1956.

Galbraith, Vivian H. *An introduction to the study of history*. London: Watts, 1964.

Gardiner, Patrick. *The nature of historical explanation*. London: Oxford University Press, 1952.

Gershoy, Leo. "Some problems of a working historian," In *Philosophy and history: a symposium*. Edited by Sidney Hook. New York: New York University Press, 1963.

Gillispie, Charles Coulston. *The edge of objectivity, an essay in the history of scientific ideas*. Princeton: Princeton University Press, 1960.

_____. *Genesis and geology, a study in the relations of scientific thought, natural theology, and social opinion in Great Britain, 1790–1850*. Cambridge: Harvard University Press, 1951.

Goldschmidt, Walter. "The anthropological study of modern society," In *International encyclopedia of the social sciences*. Edited by David L. Sills I:330–39. New York: Macmillan, 1968.

Gould, Peter R. *Spatial diffusion*. Resource Paper No. 4. Association of American Geographers: Washington, D.C., 1969.

Haebler, Konrad. *The early printers of Spain and Portugal*. London: Bibliographical Society, 1897.

_____. *The study of incunabula*. Translated from the German by Lucy Eugenia Osborne; with a foreword by Alfred W. Pollard. New York: Grolier Club, 1933.

100   Works Cited

Harnack, Carl Gustav von. *The mission and expansion of Christianity in the first three centuries.* Translated and edited by James Moffat. Second, enlarged and revised edition. 2 vols. London: W. Williams and Horgate, 1908.

Haydyn, Benjamin Vincent. *Dictionary of dates and universal information relating to all ages and nations.* New York: Putnam, 1911.

Helleiner, Karl F. "The population of Europe from the Black Death to the eve of the vital revolution," In *Cambridge Economic History of Europe,* IV: 1-94. Cambridge: Cambridge University Press, 1967.

Hempel, Carl. "The function of general laws in history," *Journal of Philosophy* 9 (1942):35-48.

Hobhouse, Leonard Trelawney; Wheeler, Gerald Clair; and Ginsberg, Morris. *The material culture and social institutions of the simpler peoples, an essay in correlations.* London: Chapman Hall, 1915.

Hodgen, Margaret T. "Geographical diffusion as a criterion of age," *American Anthropologist* 44 (1942):345-68.

_____. "Glass and paper, an historical study of acculturation," *Southwestern Journal of Anthropology* I (1945):466-97.

_____. "Similarities and dated distributions," *American Anthropologist* 52 (1950):445-65.

_____. "Anthropology, history and science," *Scientia* 87 (1952):282-87.

_____. *Change and history: A study of the dated distributions of technological innovations in England.* Viking Fund Publications in Anthropology No. 18. New York: Wenner-Gren Foundation for Anthropological Research, Inc., 1952.

_____. *Early anthropology in the sixteenth and seventeenth centuries.* Philadelphia: University of Pennsylvania Press, 1964.

_____. "Frederick John Teggart," In *International encyclopedia of the social sciences,* Edited by David L. Sills. New York: Macmillan, 1968.

Holt, William Stull. "The idea of scientific history in America," *Journal of the History of Ideas* I (1940).

Hook, Sidney. "A pragmatic criticism of the historico-genetic method," In *Essays in honor of John Dewey on the occasion of his seventieth birthday,* pp. 156-174. New York: Henry Holt, 1929.

_____. "Objectivity and reconstruction in history," In *Philosophy and history: a symposium.* Edited by Sidney Hook. New York: New York University Press, 1963.

Hozier, Henry Montague. *The invasions of England.* London: Macmillan, 1876.

Hughes, Henry Stuart. "The historians and the social scientists," *American Historical Review* 66 (1960):20-46.

_____. *History as art and as science.* New York: Harper, 1964.

The interpreter's Bible. New York: Abingdon-Cokesbury, 1954.

Jones, Arnold Hugh Martin. "The social background of the struggle between paganism and Christianity in the fourth century," In *The conflict between paganism and Christianity in the fourth century,* Essays edited by Arnaldo Momigliano. Oxford: Clarendon Press, 1963.

_____. *The later Roman empire 284-602: a social economic and administrative survey.* Norman: University of Oklahoma, 1964.

Klausner, Joseph. *From Jesus to Paul.* Translated from the Hebrew by William P. Stinespring. Boston: Beacon Press, 1961.

Kluckhohn, Clyde Kay Maben. "Developments in the field of anthropology in the 20th century," *Journal of World History* (UNESCO) III (1955):754-777.

———. "Some reflections on the method and theory of the Kulturkreislehre," *American Anthropologist* 38 (1936):157-196.

Koppers, Wilhelm. "Diffusion: transmission and acceptance," In *Current anthropology: a supplement to Anthropology Today.* Edited by William L. Thomas, Jr., pp. 169-181. Chicago: University of Chicago Press, 1956.

Kreiger, Leonard. "The horizons of history," *American Historical Review,* 63 (1957):62-74.

Kroeber, Alfred Louis. "Diffusionism," In *Encyclopedia of the Social Sciences,* V:139-142. New York: Macmillan, 1931.

———. "History and science in anthropology," *American Anthropologist* 27 (1935):539-69.

———. *Configurations of culture growth.* Berkeley: University of California Press, 1944.

———. "History and evolution," *Southwestern Journal of Anthropology* 2 (1946):1-15.

———. "What ethnography is," In *An anthropologist looks at history,* pp. 131-151. Berkeley: University of California Press, 1963.

———. "Integration of the knowledge of man," In *An anthropologist looks at history,* pp. 101-130. Berkeley: University of California Press, 1963.

———. "History and anthropology in the study of civilizations," In *An anthropologist looks at history.* Berkeley: University of California Press, 1963.

———. *Anthropology: culture patterns and processes.* New York: The Harbinger Books, Harcourt, Brace, and World, 1964.

Kuhn, Thomas S. *The structure of scientific revolutions.* Chicago: University of Chicago Press, Phoenix Editions, 1964.

Laguna, Frederica de, editor. *Selected papers from The American Anthropologist, 1888-1924.* Evanston:Illinois, 1960.

Langlois, Charles V., and Seignobos, Charles. *Introduction to the study of history.* New York: Henry Holt, 1898.

Latourette, Kenneth Scott. *A history of the expansion of Christianity: the first five centuries.* New York: Harper, 1937-45.

Levy, Marion J. and Cancian, Francesca M. "Functional analysis," In *International encyclopedia of the social sciences.* Edited by David L. Sills, VI: 21-43; I: 321-22. New York: Macmillan, 1968.

Lewis, Clive Staples. *The discarded image, an introduction to medieval and renaissance literature.* Cambridge: Cambridge University Press, 1964.

Lewontin, R. C. "The concept of social evolution," In *International encyclopedia of the social sciences.* Edited by David L. Sills, V: 202-210. New York: Macmillan, 1968.

Leyburn, James Graham. *Handbook of ethnography.* New Haven: Yale University Press, 1932.

Lindsay, T. M. "The triumph of Christianity," In *Cambridge medieval history.* Cambridge: Cambridge University Press, 1924.

Lopez, Robert Sabatino. "The trade of medieval Europe: the south," In *Cambridge Economic History of Europe,* II: 257-338. Cambridge: Cambridge University Press, 1956.

Lopez, Robert Sabatino. *The birth of Europe.* New York: Dent, 1966.
Lurie, Nancy Oestreich. "Ethnohistory: an ethnological point of view," *Ethnohistory* 8 (1961): 78–92.
Lynd, Helen M. "The nature of historical objectivity," *Journal of Philosophy* XLVII (1960): 29–43.
Mair, Lucy. "Applied anthropology," In *International encyclopedia of the social sciences.* Edited by David L. Sills, I: 325–330. New York: Macmillan, 1968.
Mandelbaum, David G. "The study of complex civilizations," In *Current anthropology: a supplement to Anthropology Today.* Edited by William L. Thomas, Jr. Chicago: University of Chicago Press, 1956.
Mandelbaum, Maurice. "Historical explanation: the problem of covering laws," *History and Theory* I (1961): 229–242.
_____. "A note on history as narrative," *History and Theory; Studies in the Philosophy of History* 6 (1967): 13–19.
Meadows, Paul. "The scientific use of historical data," *Philosophy of science* 11 (1944): 53–58.
Meer, Frederick van der. *Augustine the bishop, the life and work of a father of the church.* Translated by Brian Battershaw and G. R. Lamb. London: Sheed and Ward, 1963.
Meer, Frederick van der, and Mohrmann, Christine. *Atlas of the early Christian world.* Translated and edited by Mary F. Hedland and H. H. Rowley. London: Thomas Nelson and Sons, 1958.
Meersch, Polydore Charles van der. *Recherches sur la vie et les travauxes imprimeurs belges et neelandais.* 1856.
Momigliano, Arnaldo. "Christianity and the decline of the Roman empire," In *Conflict between paganism and Christianity.* Essays edited by Arnaldo Momigliano, pp. 1–16. Oxford: Clarendon Press, 1963.
Murdock, George Peter. "How culture changes," In *Man, culture, and society.* Edited by Harry L. Shapiro, pp. 247–260. New York: Oxford University Press, 1956.
_____. "The processing of anthropological materials," In *Readings in cross-cultural methodology.* Edited by Frank W. Moore, pp. 265–276. New Haven: HRAF Press, 1961.
_____. "The cross-cultural survey," In *Readings in cross-cultural methodology.* Edited by Frank W. Moore, pp. 45–54. New Haven: HRAF Press, 1961.
Nadel, Siegfried Ferdinand. *The foundations of social anthropology.* London: Cohen and West, 1951.
Oswald, John Clyde. *A history of printing, its development through five hundred years.* New York: Appleton, 1928.
Pareti, Luigi. *History of mankind: the ancient world 1200 BC to AD 500.* New York: Harper and Row, 1965.
Parry, J. H. "Transport and trade routes," In *The Cambridge Economic History.* Cambridge: Cambridge University Press, 1956.
Perspectives in American Indian cultures. Edited by Edward H. Spicer. Chicago: University of Chicago Press, 1961.
Postan, Michael. "The trade of medieval Europe: the north," In *Cambridge Economic History of Europe,* II: 119–251. Cambridge: Cambridge University Press, 1956.

Putnam, George Palmer. *Putnam's handbook of universal history: a series of chronological tables presenting in parallel columns, a record of the more noteworthy events in the history of the world.* . . . New York: Putnam, 1927.

Raftis, J. Ambrose. "Marc Bloch's comparative method and the rural history of medieval England," *Medieval Studies* 24 (1962): 349-368.

Ramsay, Sir William. "Roads and travel (in NT)," In *A dictionary of the Bible.* Edited by James Hastings, Extra volume pp. 375-402. New York: Scribner, 1923.

Randall, John Herman, Jr. *Nature and the historical experience.* New York: Columbia University Press, Paperback edition, 1962.

Russell, Josiah Cox. *Late ancient and medieval population.* Philadelphia: American Philosophical Society, 1958.

Sapir, Edward. *Time perspective in aboriginal American culture. A study in method.* Ottawa, Government Bureau, 1916.

Schapera, Isaac. "Should anthropologists be historians?" *Royal Anthropological Institute of Great Britain and Ireland* 65 (1962): 143-156.

Schmidt, Wilhelm. *Der ursprung der Gottesidee: Eine historisch-kritische und positiv studie* (1912), translated as the *Origin and growth of religion: Facts and theories,* by H. J. Rose. London: Methuen, 1931.

———. *Handbuch der Methode der Kultur-historischen Ethnologie* (1911), or *The culture historical method of ethnology: The scientific approach to the racial question.* Translated by S. A. Sieber. New York: Fortuny's, 1939.

———. "Primitive Man," in *European civilization and its origin and development,* by various contributors. Edited by Edward Eyre. London: Oxford University Press, 1935.

Schürer, E. "Diaspora," In *A dictionary of the Bible.* Edited by James Hastings, Extra volume. New York: Scribner, 1923.

Simpson, George Gaylord. *The geography of evolution.* Philadelphia: Chilton, 1965.

———. *This view of life: the world of an evolutionist.* New York: Harcourt, Brace and World, a Harbinger Book, 1963.

———. *The meaning of evolution: a study in the history of life and of its significance for man.* New Haven: Yale University Press, 1949.

———. *Tempo and mode in evolution.* New York: Columbia University Press, 1944.

Skeel, Caroline A. J. *Travel in the first century after Christ.* Cambridge: Cambridge University Press, 1901.

Standard Jewish Encyclopedia. Edited by Cecil Roth. London: Wit Allen, 1959.

Strong, Edward William. "How is practice of history tied to theory?" *Journal of Philosophy* 46 (1949): 637-44.

Strong, William Duncan. "Anthropological theory and archeological fact," In *Essays in anthropology presented to A. L. Kroeber.* Berkeley: University of California Press, 1936.

———. "Historical approach in anthropology," In *Anthropology today: an encyclopedic inventory.* Chicago, University of Chicago Press, 1953.

Sturtevant, William C. "Anthropology, history, and ethnohistory," *Ethnohistory* 13 (1966): 1-51.

Teggart, Frederick John. "Anthropology and history," *Journal of Philosophy* 16 (1919): 691-96.

──────. "The humanistic study of change in time," *Journal of Philosophy* 23 (1926): 309-15.

──────. "Spengler," *Saturday Review of Literature* 5 (1929): 597-99.

──────. "Notes on 'timeless' sociology, a discussion," *Social Forces* VII (1929): 362-65.

──────. *Rome and China: a study in correlations in historical events*. Berkeley: University of California Press, 1939.

──────. *Theory and processes of history*. Berkeley: University of California Press, 1941.

──────. *The idea of progress, a collection of readings*. Revised edition with an introduction by George H. Hildebrand. Berkeley: University of California Press, 1949.

Tennant, Frederick Robert. "Natural law," In *Hastings encyclopedia of religion and ethics*, IX. New York: Scribner, 1925.

Theory and practice in historical study: a report of the committee on historiography. Social Science Research Council, Bulletin 54. New York: 1946.

The social sciences in historical study. A report of the committee on historiography. Social Science Research Council, Bulletin 64. New York: 1954.

Thomas, Keith. "Anthropology and history," *Past and Present* 24 (1963): 3-24.

Thompson, E. A. "Christianity and the northern barbarians," *Nottingham Medieval Studies* I (1957):3-21.

──────. "Christianity and the northern barbarians," In *The conflict between paganism and Christianity in the fourth century*. Essays edited by Arnaldo Momigliano. Oxford: Clarendon Press, 1963.

Tylor, Sir Edward Burnett. *Primitive culture: researches into the development of mythology, philosophy, religion, language, art, and custom*. New York: Brentano's, 1924.

Uhlendorf, Bernard Alexander. "The invention of printing and its spread until 1470," *Library Quarterly* II (1932): 179-231.

Warmington, B. H. *The North African provinces from Diocletian to the Vandal conquest*. Cambridge: Cambridge University Press, 1954.

Wedgwood, Cicely Veronica. "History and the imagination," In *Truth and opinion: historical essays*. London: Collins, 1960.

White, Morton Gabriel. "Historical explanation," *Mind* (1943): 212-29.

Willis, John Christopher. *Age and area: a study in geographical distribution and origin of species*. Cambridge: Cambridge University Press, 1922.

Zilsel, Edgar. "Physics and the problems of historico-sociological laws," *Philosophy of Science* 8 (1941).

Index

Adeney, Walter H., 53
Africa, congregations in North, 57, 62, 77, 81-82, 89-90
Age and Area, 4-5, 8, 30, 31, 34, 62; radiation from center, 62, 89; geographical criteria of age, 82. *See also* Diffusion, Kulturkreis theory
Anderson, Robert T., 4
Angus, Samuel, 71, 73
Anthropology, study of as a natural science, 3, 34-35; as confined to atypical human sample, 33; in relation to life sciences, geology, 2; as descriptive, 2-3; as administrative or applied, 17, 20; in relation to history, 24-26, 28-30, 34-35; on likeness to history, 2, 4, 26, 96. *See* Ethnohistory; Events, dated; Kroeber; Evans-Pritchard.

Bagley, Philip, 26
Barnett, Homer Garner, 19-21
Beard, Charles Arthur, 10, 35
Becker, Carl Lotus, 12, 35
Bennett, Henry Stanley, 71
Berlin, Isaiah, 11, 35
Bidney, David, 8, 14, 16, 24, 25, 65, 67, 68, 95
Bloch, Marc, 6, 66
Boas, Franz, 16, 24, 28
Boas, George, 19, 67
Bock, Kenneth E., 4, 8, 29, 66
Brinton, Crane, 36
Bühler, Curt Ferdinand, 46, 71
Burrow, John Wyon, 66

Carr, Edward Hallett, 8, 35
Clair, Colin, 77
Changes, dated cultural, collection of, 38, 53-58, 66; two options: changes already assembled, 42-44; assembled de novo, 42; by Teggart, 38-39; by Kuhn, 39-40; types of presses and congregations, their exhaustiveness, 44; of collectors, 43-44; classification of, 9, 13, 42-62; rates of changes, 47-48, 50-51, 57; geographical features, 45-59. *See* Clusters, Distance acceptance at a: temporal and geographical distributions of, 42-64; distributions, common features of, 64; correlations of, 44, 66, 77; westerly direction of, 53, 57; significance of foreign born as carriers, 73-77, 78, 86, 93; named initiators, 73, 80; transportation, 83-89; urbanism, 89-93
Civilization, problem of, 3, 4, 95; according to Tylor, 4; according to Kroeber, 25, 27-28
Classification. *See* Changes, dated cultural
Clustering, 56, 57, 59, 64, 77, 84
Collection. *See* Changes, dated cultural
Comparative or Historical Method, 3-4; definition by Comte, 28 n. 54, 29; distinction from comparison, 28 n. 54, 65-66; see Teggart on; see Bock on
Comparison, 11, 12, 13, 40, 95; resist-